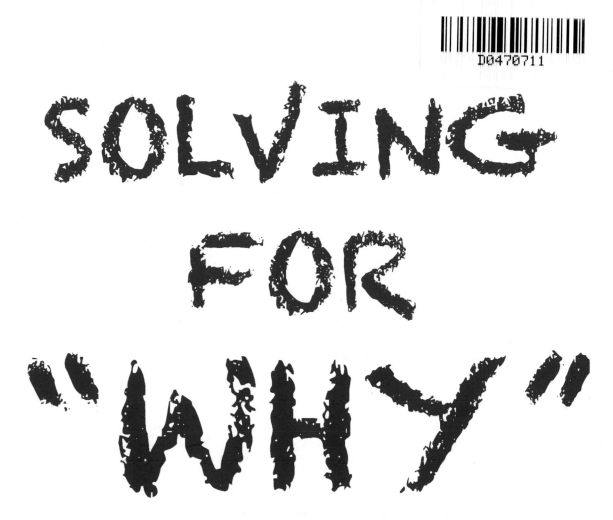

SOLVING FOR "WHY"

A Guide to Creating Meaning, Community, and Purpose in Your Higher Education Experience

ANTONIUS TSAI

Solving for "WHY"

**A Guide to Creating Meaning, Community, and Purpose
in Your Higher Education Experience**

SolvingforWhy.com
Copyright © 2018 by Antonius Tsai
Cover & Interior Illustration by XCEL Creative
Cover Design by XCEL Creative

Print ISBN: 978-1-54393-810-4

eBook ISBN: 978-1-54393-811-1

Printed in the United States of America
SolvingforWhy.com

Dedicated to Bob Malkovsky,
my high school physics teacher.
What you taught me, I have learned.

ACKNOWLEDGMENTS

To the students that I had the honor to work with. I wake up each morning and go to work with joy knowing that we will have some few precious moments in the day to learn together! Thank you for those moments.

To my lovely and brilliant wife Angie, whom I adore above all else. You listened with love and patience to my rambling musings on education. Those musings, over time, mixed with your loving presence, became my message.

To my mom, who had unconditional confidence in me. You are the sun and I am the blade of grass growing towards the stars.

To my dad, who is the most generous person I have known. You demonstrated through your life, the indispensable value of love and community.

To my colleagues in education at Utah, especially Tom Hurtado, Sara Lamb, Adam Stevenson, Boyd Richards, Janet Lindsley, Megan Fix, Jim Agutter, Wendy Hobson-Rohrer, Wayne Samuelson, Rory Hume, and Vivian Lee. We all share the same dream.

To my colleagues from the RWJFCSP program, especially Tammy Chang, Rod Hayward, Michelle Moniz, and Elizabeth Patton. You have seen when this idea was just a drawing on a napkin from Angelos. Thank you for your faith and friendship in this journey from the beginning.

To my colleagues at the University of Michigan Medical School, especially Raj Mangrukar, Paticia Mullan, Mike Englesbe, and Chris Chapman. I greatly valued our time together, discussing and working on what medical education could be. Raj, our friendship and professional collaboration is a source of inspiration for me. This book serves as a sign of my commitment to our kindred purpose in education.

To my colleagues at the Ross School of Busines at the University of Michigan (Go Blue!), epseically Leslie Lynn, Leslie Mulder, Al Cotrone, and Bob Quinn. Through our discussions, I have learned much about how to unlock the potential in others and to imagine what higher education could be like if we all approached our work in that spirit.

To Josh Hanagarne, Amanda Johnson, and Dan Mulhern who helped to shape and clarify the message in the book. This book contains your voices and imagery. Thank you for your collaboration and guidance during this process. I'm proud of the work that we have done together.

To the Divine, whose expression through life is the source of all meaning, community, and purpose.

With Gratitude,

Salt Lake City, Utah
May 2018

CONTENTS

INTRODUCTION

1:37 am? Wow, did I really just play six hours of video games? I shifted my gaze from the clock on the dorm room wall back to the screen. *I was hoping to get a little bit of finance studying in, but it's too late tonight. Hopefully, I can still get to bed by 2:30 am.*

There was a little bit of video gaming to finish up, so I took a swig from my can of Mountain Dew and set it down on the nightstand next to me.

I'll study in the morning, I decided as I deftly tapped keys on my computer to pilot the fighter jet on the screen. *There are lectures tomorrow at 9:00 am and 10:30 am, but I was already planning to skip them.*

I had been skipping lectures since I was a freshman. What was the point of sitting there in a class of 300 people, taking notes on things like "internal rate of return" when I could just read it in a book and pass the test?

What is the relevance of any of this anyway? To get a job? I guess. I mean, that's what a lot of the people around me are all excited to do, but it makes no sense to me.

Earlier that night, I'd had dinner with a classmate who told me that he was hoping to land a job with one of the Big 8 (back then) accounting firms.

"That'll set you up well for a career in business or finance," he said, as if encouraging me to pursue the same path.

Yeah, but what if you don't really know what you want, except that you don't want finance? I wondered to myself quietly. *He seems to have a direction at least—something I wish I had.*

It was the second semester of my sophomore year at an Ivy League university, with a top-rated business program, but I was burnt out with school.

I was good enough at taking tests that I wasn't going to fail out. I was an Asian kid, after all, and to fail out would be completely unthinkable. So, I put in just enough effort to maintain a GPA above 3.0.

Ugh. 2:09 am. I glanced back at the clock. *I better get to bed. But why? What's to stop me from playing video games all night? Why the hell am I doing any of this? I'm not "learning" anything except how to master playing video games alone.* I shook my head at the reality. *But I can't drop out. My parents would be so disappointed and I would be a complete embarrassment to everyone.*

I turned the monitor off, dropped into my bed, and stared up at the ceiling.

I have two more years of this? What am I going to do? This is NOT what I hoped it would be. I know I should be grateful that I'm here and on the path toward a "great career," but I'm not. What is the matter with me anyway?

I drifted off to sleep so that I could wake up and continue drifting through school and life.

THE RISE AND FALL OF EXPECTIONS

My parents had placed education as the top priority for me and my brother at a very young age. We grew up in Taiwan where education was a serious endeavor, and I dutifully memorized my multiplication tables and practiced my Chinese characters. In my elementary school, we were not allowed to run during recess or to talk in a loud voice. Education was serious.

When I was eight, my family moved to the U.S. where I attended third grade in the suburbs of Philadelphia and had a very different experience. We enjoyed milk and cookies. We played board games. The teacher read stories to us. It was all quite a shock, in a good way. I didn't realize that education could be so much fun!

Over time, however, education became more serious again. There were more facts to memorize and the tests became more important. But that was okay. I was a good student who could memorize stuff and take tests. The tempo of memorizing and test-taking picked up in middle school and high school, and the guidance counselors started talking about class rank and college applications. To a high school kid, getting into a good college was important, so I applied myself and got good grades and was voted "most intelligent" by my classmates. That was a cool distinction to have, although it didn't translate into many dates with girls.

Toward the end of high school, I noticed that I was getting "tired" of school. I was getting tired of memorizing facts for tests. I was tired of trying to get good grades. What was the point of school? Oh yes, to get into a good college. Maybe college would be different?

Eventually, I did get into a good college. I had such high expectations. Wouldn't you if, for the last twelve years, everybody in your life talked it up as the ultimate achievement? I was sure I'd make so many new friends and enjoy many interesting classes. I believed I would finally "find myself."

But none of those things happened.

Most of my classes in the first two years were held in giant lecture halls with 300 other students. At least in high school, I knew my teachers and classmates and didn't feel completely lost in rooms of hundreds of strangers.

Hoping to befriend other smart kids like me, I was disappointed by the massive game of musical chairs, played with popularity as the main criteria. An early casualty, I never really found my "tribe."

The program that I matriculated with was business. My parents felt that it was very practical. Business can mean a lot of different things, and I was hoping that the school could help translate this academic major into something that had meaning for me. I was a curious person. I wanted to contribute. However, I couldn't see how getting a job in accounting at Price Waterhouse could make me happy.

Where else could I turn for meaning and purpose?

Despairing, I was ready to give up and figure out how to get paid to play video games when a life-changing opportunity came my way—a class called "Military Science."

I'd developed a specialty in history and helped win a quiz bowl in high school, and I thought I'd enjoy learning more about the military since I'd really enjoyed studying the wars. Well, it turned out that the class was actually Reserve Officers Training Corps (ROTC).

I never thought I'd be a solider, but when the military recruiter mentioned that the Army would pay for tuition, I thought, *Well, if I paid my own way through college, then I can get whatever grades I want.* That was the immature, desperate, and questionable logic of the nineteen-year-old me.

Fortunately for me, ROTC was the first answer to my desperate search for meaning. In fact, I got more out of the ROTC experience than the rest of my college classes combined. We went out to the field where, in the cold and with little sleep, I learned just how much I could push myself to do. More importantly, I was instantly connected to a network of people who cared for me, and for whom I had a responsibility to care for in return. We talked of "service," "leadership," and "sacrifice"— meaningful concepts not taught in my business classes.

It was like living in two different worlds. There was one world of classes and quizzes and grades which was nominally called "education," and this other world of marching, tactical field exercises, and physical training.

This new world didn't resemble education, but it taught me the most important concepts I needed to know and gave me opportunities to embody them.

SOLVING FOR eXPERTISE + eXCELLENCE

Universities offer external knowledge. Want to know how to write a research paper? You're in the right place. Want to know what kind of career would be most meaningful to you? Nope. Guidance and developmental mentoring just aren't what they do. It's not that they're hostile to the idea, but they're still aggressively bad at it. Unless you're in a philosophy class, the chances that your studies will force you to ask yourself tough questions about personal meaning are slim to none.

Universities operate by a pretty simple formula:

External knowledge transferred to student = Education.

You may be too young to remember well, but information used to be scarce. Or at least, there were barriers to finding it. It was locked away in the heads of professors, or librarians, or buried in archives that could only be accessed with a student ID. Back then, it was easier to call information a valuable asset and charge for it. The Internet changed all of that. The amount of information that anyone can access is staggering. In economics, when something is plentiful, it becomes a commodity. Universities are still in the business of providing knowledge, but that commodity is no longer scarce.

Should you learn the knowledge taught in colleges? Sure, particularly if you're studying something with high stakes. If you're my accountant, I don't want you consulting a Magic 8 Ball to untangle some financial disaster for me or plan my investment strategy. I want you to measure it against the body of knowledge you gained and make the most informed, educated decision possible. If you're my surgeon, I don't you waxing poetic with a scalpel when sticking to standardized medical knowledge would do. Plenty of information learned in college is useful or necessary once you graduate. However, it's important to know that because information *is* a commodity, focusing your sole attention on it while in school will not yield you much value in your development.

They teach in academies far too many things, and far too much that is useless.
~ Johanne Wolfgang von Goethe

STANDARDIZING...PEOPLE?

The industrial revolution brought us the mass production paradigm, and the idea that there are laborers, managers, and the capability to produce a ton of stuff with increasingly little human effort. In this model, the manager's job is to maximize production, and maximum production requires standardization to make sure things are cracking along efficiently. Inefficiency equals waste, and waste equals a loss of profits. So, managers need to standardize. In theory, they must know "A" so they can get "B" out of their employees and for their company.

As far as business goes, this is a great model. When someone buys a standardized product, they already know what they're buying. The fact that it's standardized is part of the appeal! If you bought an iPhone with nine buttons and a bunch of knobs that had to be twisted, you'd wonder who went insane and deviated from Apple's world domination strategy.

In the same way, colleges must measure things to make sure people achieve the expertise and excellence they need to execute their functions in their future career, and external knowledge is easy to measure. Tests, grades, rankings, credits, etc. These are not abstractions because numbers can be attached to them.

But…internal worth? Subjective measures? Nah. Those don't come with your degree unless you take part in some serious introspection. If you sit in a lecture hall with 300 other students, and you're all learning the same thing, are you discovering what makes you unique? Probably not. This isn't to disparage the worth of facts, but meaning doesn't come from facts.

> What we do not—should not, must not—want, is standardized people, and universities are currently in the building sameness.

Students are more than their grades. Accountants are more than their knowledge of financial conventions. Doctors are more than the medical facts they know and procedures they can perform. You are more than what you learn in class.

There's something unique in you.

REPLACING EXPECTATIONS WITH EXPERIENCE

In my subsequent experiences inside and outside of higher education, I began to understand what had been missing in my college experience. In fact, I quickly realized that what was missing was not just missing for me, but for many students who are going through the process of higher education—from college students to masters-level students to post-docs.

After my service in the Army, where I learned to take charge of a platoon and then a company of 350 soldiers, I returned to business school to get my MBA and was stunned by how different my experience was.

Not so much the content. Finance was still finance. Marketing was still marketing. However, something was different *within* me, which allowed me to experience business school the second time around completely differently.

For one thing, I knew myself better. In college, I was only responsible for myself. In the real world, other people were counting on me. I'd had to be responsible for the training, welfare, and performance of hundreds of people. That had pushed me, and I'd learned my true capacity beyond taking a test for a grade. So when I returned to school, I wasn't targeting grades. It was a real privilege to be a student again, and to attend class for the sake of learning was liberating.

Secondly, the business school was set up in cohorts of sixty students who took the same classes together in the first year. While that wasn't exactly the same level of intimacy as sharing a foxhole, it promoted a sense of common identity among students within the cohort. With that as our common ground, we gradually learned more about one another and eventually could even anticipate what others would say when someone raised their hand in class. That sense of belonging filled the same place in me that being part of a platoon had.

Lastly, I had a better sense of what I wanted to do with my career. In the Army, when not deployed, we were consistently training; and at some point, I had realized that I enjoyed training soldiers—that I actually enjoyed being an educator. When I got to business school, I found ways to help and teach others. In fact, in my second year, I was individually tutoring sixty other business school students. The b-school also allowed us to take two electives outside the b-school, and I took mine at Teacher's College across the street from the b-school. Suddenly, I had a vision of being in education, and that purpose gave me a bigger reason to learn.

Whereas higher education is often focused on the *WHAT* and the *HOW* of things, I would say that the key difference between my two business school experiences was about the *WHY*, which included the domains of meaning, community, and purpose.

I believe these are the three core desires of every student in higher education, and my experience over the last few decades has not only proven this to be true, but shown me the negative impact of not Solving for WHY in higher education:

When I was a **Corporate Recruiter,** I saw very smart young people struggle to communicate who they are. The went to great schools. They had great resumes and grades. Yet when they talked about themselves, they sounded generic. They were all trying to say what they thought we wanted to hear. They were all looking to conform to that "formula" for success.

As a **Business School Career Advisor**, I worked with students looking to find meaning, community, and purpose in their lives. Should this student work at an investment bank or start a restaurant? What were their values around work and family? How would they negotiate their salary as related to how much they valued their time? These were among the many topics not covered in class, but invaluable to their education.

When I became a **Faculty Member**, I taught classes on international business cultures (b-school) and leadership development (med school). These experiences further taught me the challenges of "teaching" meaning, community, and purpose. It's not easy. The trap is to tell others what you know, but how do you teach it in a way that promotes the students' sense of *WHY*? Solving for X in an algebraic equation is a process that can be taught quickly and then practiced, but this *WHY* business requires deep self-reflection and the opportunity to embody one's learning.

For the last few years, I've been teaching leadership development in a way that makes up for the lack of attention given to the most important *WHY* questions in our education system. Today, as a **University Administrator**, I work with education leaders to incorporate meaning, community, and purpose into education. My focus is on helping young adults ask the *WHY* questions, follow the curiosity and wonder that we all had as children, and acquire the self-knowledge and life skills they need to create meaning in their lives and enjoy the sense of belonging and self-confidence that comes from doing so.

This book is the result of my desire to bring this conversation to other universities and graduate schools so that students can gain access to this other half of education.

SOLVING FOR WHY = THE OTHER SIDE OF THE EQUATION

Universities are more like…supermarkets, and if you've been in a few, you know not all supermarkets are created equal. They vary in size, products, and volume; but one thing they have in common is variety. And there's something else. If you go into a supermarket when you're hungry—whether you are in a high-end or bargain basement supermarket—you'll leave with more than you should have, and you'll make choices based on appetite, impulse, and uncertainty.

You have a responsibility as a shopper, whether you're shopping for food or education. Smart shoppers have a shopping list, but you won't get what you want out of a university if you don't *know* what you want. And you can't trust the administrators and teachers to get it right for you.

So, how do you do it?

Here are the questions that contain all of the others: What do you want? Do you really want it, or does it just *seem* like what you want, or what other people want you to want? It's possible that you haven't ever really thought about this, but honest and open reflection about this will change your life. You might say that you want good grades, a rowdy, fun circle of friends, interesting classes, to graduate at the top, to leave with an excellent job in hand, to go to grad school, or all of the above.

There's nothing wrong with any of these. But they're generic. Anyone could want them. Most people in college probably do want them. So, some of the things that you probably want aren't unique; they aren't what YOU really want, but some of the things that have been wanted and expected for you.

As you enter young adulthood, your identity is entwined with social norms and expectations. You are led by outer voices for a time because your inner voice is not strong enough yet. You aren't the author of your own story, but you can be.

I've been working on these issues for years, and I've found that no matter what they say, people really want three uniquely-defined things: meaning, community, and purpose.

What you want, what I want, what everyone wants, is…

To contribute your unique gift... (Meaning)

You can do things no one else can because you are someone that no one else is. The combination of your attributes, skills, thoughts, experiences, motivations, and actions, both current and future, means there is something that *only you* can give to the world. Whatever your unique gift is, the world is poorer without it. That's why it's not only in your best interest to discover it, but you have an *obligation* to discover it and use it to help people. This is one of those great opportunities where focusing on yourself with all your might could be the thing that makes you most useful to the world.

...while finding belonging in a caring community... (Community)

We're social animals. Consider that in the entire animal kingdom, it's pretty much only humans that share food. We gather, on purpose, night after night, to do something that's unheard of in nature. Community matters to us, no matter how misanthropic or anti-social someone might seem or claim to be. We need each other to be our best. Once you find yourself in the right community for you, you'll be in the enviable spot of having people that work to make your life better, and who give you a chance to do the same for them. If there is anything like an ideal society, it lies somewhere in that direction.

...to something meaningful that is greater than yourself. (Purpose)

I'm not one to obsess over legacies, but I do believe that we can all make a mark here while we're on earth. Can you think of a better use of our time than to reduce unnecessary suffering in the world? Or fight ignorance, particularly our own? When we know ourselves as well as possible, we can finally start to get a glimpse of what true meaning actually looks like—working on the meaning of our own lives, in service of life as a whole.

Your WHY = Meaning + Community + Purpose

These things aren't dependent on external knowledge, lists of facts, or final exams. And even though everyone seems to want meaning, community, and purpose, there are an infinite number of ways in which to express and experience them. That's what makes them aspects of your unique personality. They'll look like what you intend them to be, if you put in the time to think about what they mean to you.

If you don't find meaning in college, it's your responsibility. Your life is your life. There's no one to blame. But also, no one else gets to take credit for your success. The most rewarding successes will be the result of the inner work that is the real labor of life.

Why did Mark Zuckerberg drop out of school? Because once he found his purpose, he could follow his own path. That's the goal beyond just getting through college. I'm not encouraging you to drop out of college, but to prioritize the inner work over the external.

This book will help you do that. This is the book I wish I'd had when I went to college. Following its message will hopefully lead you to a more meaningful and purposeful life—a good life. Not someone else's idea of good, but yours.

HOW TO READ THIS BOOK

You'll see that this book is designed to guide you through the process of solving for your *WHY*. In this equation, we must first solve for the three domains of meaning, community, and purpose; and there are multiple variables for each of these domains which are elaborated upon in each chapter.

I've shared stories of students—students who I work with regularly to help them solve for *WHY*—to show you that you're not alone and also to give you examples of why and how these questions are important to your life or will be some day. I've also included many personal stories to show the personal nature of gaining insight through life experience.

NOTE: Although most of the student stories I've included involve medical or business students, the underlying concepts and questions for your reflection are applicable to learners in any discipline and at any level, including undergraduate, graduate, and professional.

Also, at the end of each chapter, I've included some "Word Problems" to help you find your own answers. You may find it useful to reflect and process the content in each chapter before moving on. You may also consider working through the questions and content in groups or with a coach or advisor.

You may find that as you progress in your studies and in your career, your answers to the questions posed in this book evolve. Your answers may change, but the questions stay the same. You'll want to return to these questions on a regular basis (even beyond your time as a student) to maintain your connection with your *WHY*.

It's not enough to solve for X. You need to solve for *WHY*, and this is a powerful way to do it.

I would contend that the most impactful classes that you've experienced "transformed" you in some way. These were classrooms where you didn't just memorize more information, to be forgotten later. You grew on the inside, and you left the class more grounded and connected with your "self."

This is my goal for every class I teach. In fact, in the leadership course, I often started the first day of class with this prompt for the students to reflect upon: "What is most important to you?"

The uncomfortable realization for many was that they didn't have an answer. Another realization was that, despite being among the most highly educated people in society, their education had not shed much light on this very basic question. In fact, many students came up to me to say that this was the first time in their higher education career (after undergrad, after medical school, after residency training) that they were asked to consider this fundamental question.

Interesting. After so many years of "education," there were some very essential lessons which were almost completely absent.

The "Hidden Half" of Education

We all know the part of education that deals with knowledge. What is the capital of France? What is the boiling point of water? Who wrote *A Tale of Two Cities*?

We all know the part of education that deals with skills. How do you write a five-paragraph essay? How do you solve for X in a math equation? How do you set up an experiment to test a hypothesis?

When we think about education, we generally think about knowledge and skills, but that is only half of a truly effective education formula.

All I had to do to learn this hard lesson was teach my first Leadership course for a group of doctors who had finished residency and were training for careers in health policy research. When their former instructor had retired, I was invited to step in.

"What about Leadership do you want me to teach?" I asked the administration.

They gave me a list of skills that, to them, added up to something called leadership: negotiation, giving difficult feedback, cultivating mentors, managing staff, and getting promoted.

So, I started to teach those skills, but something was…wrong. To say that the feedback wasn't glowing would be charitable. The students (doctors) didn't feel like it was turning them into leaders. I didn't either. We were all correct.

Up to that point, I had considered myself a rather good instructor, and those class evaluations were devastating. They forced me to re-examine my whole approach to "teaching" leadership. During this process of introspection, I came across this quote by Peter Drucker:[1]

Management is doing things right; leadership is doing the right things.

That quote struck me like a lightning bolt. I quickly realized that most of what was conventionally considered leadership was actually closer to expertise. Knowing *HOW* to do something can make you an expert, but experts are kind of like walking versions of the Internet in a specific niche—an authority—but that doesn't necessarily mean anything except that they know a lot of facts. That list of skills that I had taught focused completely on the *HOW* to do things.

But how many leadership development classes did people like Abraham Lincoln, Gandhi, Mother Theresa, or Martin Luther King, Jr., take to be able to do the things they did? They were not experts, but leaders. They were not focused on "doing things right," but on "doing the right things." They were not focused on the *HOW* but the *WHY*.

Because I was focused solely on teaching the *HOW*, I had become part of the machine. I had to find another way. But how to teach the *WHY*?

Eventually, I realized that Drucker's distinction between management and leadership can also apply to the *HOW* and the *WHY* of education. Higher education is obsessed with knowledge and skills, and operates on the assumption that education is about the transfer of that knowledge and the development of those skills. It is focused almost entirely on the *HOW*.

To contrast the part of education that deals with *HOW* (knowledge and skills) with the part that deals with the *WHY*, let's call that part "meaning and purpose."

Simply, let's suppose education consists of these two halves. (see diagram below)

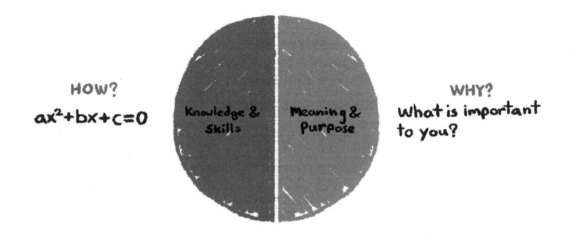

I got some very frightening responses when I showed this diagram to my students and posed the question: "Think back to all your formal schooling and training. What percentage of the time was devoted to acquiring knowledge and skills? What percentage of the time was devoted to cultivating meaning and purpose?" On average, they agreed: 98% on knowledge and skills, 2% on meaning and purpose.

What about you? Where has the focus of your education been? On the *HOW*, or the *WHY*?

If you go to college and pay your tuition (perhaps borrowing a hefty sum in the process), you expect that by the time you graduate that you would have mastered some domain of knowledge and/or skill. That's a reasonable expectation. How come we don't have those same expectations about meaning and purpose? Would it not be reasonable that, by the time you graduate college or other higher education program, you would have significantly honed and expanded your sense of purpose? Of knowing yourself and what is most important to you?

There's a great quote by Antoine de Saint-Exupery, the author of *The Little Prince*.

> *If you want to build a ship, don't drum up people together to collect wood and don't assign them tasks and work, but rather teach them to long for the endless immensity of the sea.*

How much of higher education is about learning how to chop wood or, perhaps more apt, the theory of wood chopping taught by PhDs in wood chopping.

More importantly, how much of higher education could be about "creating a longing for the sea"?

What if higher education provided both?

The HOW of the WHY: Clarity Through Reflection

Unlike the *HOW*, which you must acquire from external sources, the *WHY* you must get from within. You can read books about purpose, but that doesn't give you purpose.

I think it's worth digging a little deeper into our assumptions here. As students, many of us assumed that if we read about a lot of topics, got involved in a lot of activities, and got good grades, then our purpose would become clear. If we sampled a lot of things and excelled at something, then we would know what we should do with our life. Right?

Well, let's take another walk down the aisle in the grocery store. Have you ever gone to the store hungry, but without a clear sense of what you wanted? What did you come back with—some Doritos and Hot Pockets?

On the other hand, have you ever gone to the grocery store and come back with exactly the things that you had intended? What was the difference? The difference was likely that you had set clearer intentions the time where you came back with the right things. Perhaps you were baking a cake and needed certain ingredients. Perhaps you had set boundaries about the kind of food that you were going to buy.

The same concept holds with higher education. If what you have is a "hunger for success" and you go to a university without reflecting on your intent, who knows what you will come out with! You must reflect and set some intentions prior and during the education experience so that what you come out with is in line with what you really want.

To get clarity on your purpose, you must reflect.

But…how does one reflect on the intention to get clarity? What kind of questions should one ask oneself?

Below are some questions which may be useful. (This is not an exhaustive list.)

- Who do I intend to be?
- What matters most to me?
- What is my superpower?
- How do others see me, and how do I see myself?
- How will I show up for others?
- What kind of people do I need to know?
- What's my way to build connection with others?
- How do I communicate with influence?
- How do I contribute to the world around me?
- What am I committed to that is greater than myself?
- How will I define success?
- What is my next step?

As an example, let's think about the question: "What kind of people do I need to know?"

When I had a chance to interview many graduates from the programs I was associated with, I had them reflect on something they wished they had done more of during school. One of the most common answers I heard was that they wished that they had reached out and met more people.

School goes by fast and sometimes you need to set intentions early on so that you don't wake up on graduation day, wondering where the last several years have gone and what you have to show for them. What if, at the beginning of school, you had set the intention that you would make ten good friends and develop three great mentoring relationships? Just setting that intention and maintaining attention on it will greatly increase the chances that you will actually walk away from school with friends and mentors.

It is your answers to questions that clarify your intent, that will help you define your sense of meaning, community, and purpose.

The Three Domains: MEANING, COMMUNITY, and PURPOSE

Some time ago, as I was re-developing my course on leadership, I examined a number of frameworks on the topic. One of the insights that many frameworks pointed out was the management versus leadership dichotomy, which led to the afore-mentioned "two halves" concept when applied to education.

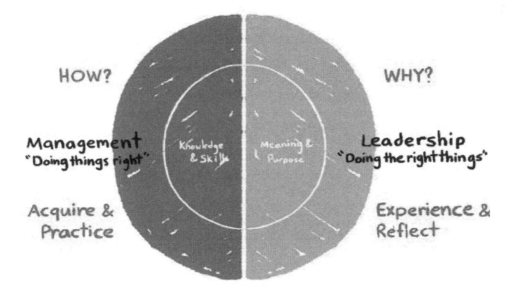

One key distinction between the knowledge and skills half and the meaning and purpose half is that meaning and purpose is not something you acquire from a book. You develop it through reflection on your experiences. You can't read about whether you prefer pizza or foie gras. You must experience eating them and reflect on your preference. Very often, we read that "many people like pizza," so therefore we think we should like pizza.

So, if we need to reflect, what do we reflect upon?

Just like many of the leadership frameworks point out the "two halves," they also highlight three domains. Why these three domains? Why not four domains? Why not twenty-three domains?

Let's take a definition of leadership from a notable leadership scholar, Peter Northouse:[2]

Leadership is a process whereby an individual influences a group of individuals to achieve a common goal.

If we were to break down this definition, we'd find that there are three elements.

- **"An Individual…"** This is the part about the "inner" domain of the leader. This domain deals with the values, the capacity, and the motives of the leader. It is the first-person, "intrapersonal" aspect.

- **"…influences a group of individuals…"** In order to have leadership, you must have leaders and you must have followers. The leader does not do everything him or herself. The leader *influences* action on the part of others. This domain deals with the influence of the leader on others. It is the second-person, "interpersonal" aspect.

- **"…to achieve a common goal."** The leader doesn't influence people for no reason, but the influence is aimed at people taking action towards a goal of the group. This domain deals with purpose, goals, and process. It is the third-person, "extrapersonal" aspect.

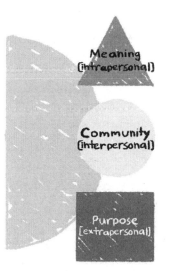

If we were to overlay the concepts of meaning, community, and purpose with the three domains of intrapersonal, interpersonal, and extrapersonal, it may look like the following:

Domain: Meaning / Intrapersonal

Domain: Community / Interpersonal

Domain: Purpose / Extrapersonal

The questions for reflection are powerful when they align with one of the three domains of meaning, community, or purpose. Whether it be for a leader or for a "regular" person, in order to form a comprehensive picture, we must select a set of questions which cover all three domains.

How might the list of questions from earlier in the chapter—questions like, "What kind of people do I need to know?"—fit into these three domains?

Domain: MEANING *(Intrapersonal)* Who do I intend to be?	VARIABLES in the MEANING domain **Values:** *What matters most to me?* (Variable 1) **Strengths:** *What is my superpower?* (Variable 2) **Self-Awareness:** *How do others see me, and how do I see myself?* (Variable 3)

Domain: COMMUNITY *(Interpersonal)* How will I show up for others?	VARIABLES in the COMMUNITY domain **Network:** *What kind of people do I need to know?* (Variable 4) **Relationships:** *What's my way to build connection with others?* (Variable 5) **Communication:** *How do I communicate with influence?* (Variable 6)

Domain: PURPOSE *(Extrapersonal)* How will I contribute to the world around me?	VARIABLES in the PURPOSE domain **Mission:** *What am I committed to that is greater than myself?* (Variable 7) **Vision:** *How will I define success?* (Variable 8) **Process:** *What is my next step?* (Variable 9)

Your WHY = Meaning + Community + Purpose

In the following chapters, this book will examine the three domains of meaning, community, and purpose in detail, providing opportunities for you to consider these questions and develop answers, which will give you a richer understanding of meaning, community, and purpose and facilitate your ability to create them in your own life.

Ready?

DOMAIN:
MEANING

- - - - - - - - - -

WHO DO I INTEND TO BE?

*Definitions belonged to the
definers - not the defined.*

~ TONI MORRISON

Who do I intend to be?

Authenticity vs Imitation: Stand for Something

If you're reading this, it means that the lights are on. Your lights. And if you're reading this, you probably want to *be* something, but you may not know exactly what. Maybe the answer you have been giving isn't working for you anymore. Maybe you simply want to feel an aspiration that isn't currently there.

"What do you want to be when you grow up?" The question is actually more complex than it appears. Let's just look at it from a career perspective, since you'll also likely have a career. Do you want to be a doctor? A lawyer? A teacher? An engineer? A consultant?

It's easier in the beginning to identify oneself with a career path than to wrestle with the full meaning to the question of, "Who am I?" So let's say you want to become a lawyer. You go to law school with 300 other aspiring lawyers. You attend the same classes as your 300 other classmates. You do the same assignments. You acquire the same degree.

Fast forward, ten years.

You go to a class reunion. You see that some people are happy and some people are miserable. Some people find their lives meaningful, and some people are struggling to find meaning. Some people are happily married and some people are divorced. Did you hear that one person is even in jail? Oh my.

Why is there such variation? After all, you were mostly of the same intelligence. You all received roughly the same education. You all did become lawyers.

For a while, I fell into the same mindset. I went to a great school and got a high-paying job. I had what anyone would call a comfortable lifestyle. And you know what? It didn't matter. It's not that I wasn't grateful, but it seemed like having these nice things should have mattered more.

In hindsight, was it really enough to say that you wanted to be a lawyer? What did you *really* want?

It would take time for me to see it, but I really didn't want to conform. Who does? I wanted to stand out. I wanted to be unique, and useful, and to do the things that no one else could do. It's tough to feel irreplaceable if you're marching in lock-step like everyone else. Taken to its most ridiculous extreme, conformity is the stuff of every dystopian future ever imagined by science fiction writers. "What if everyone was the same?" is a question that should make us shudder.

For all the lawyers out there, they contribute at different levels. Some are barely scraping by while others are contributing at the top of their game. They have influence. They are sought after. They have found their unique way of contributing.

In the statement below, in dealing within the domain of meaning, we are not merely looking for a generic life or career path. We are looking to be authentic to our unique self and to *contribute our unique gift*.

Meaning → Community ↙

To contribute your unique gift, while finding belonging in a caring community, to something meaningful that is greater than yourself.

↖ Purpose

If you *were* to be a lawyer, what would the best version of that look like for you?

The answer will unlikely come from a blinding flash of epiphany. It will emerge over time as you live your life while holding on to the question: "Who do I intend to be?"

If we are anything, I think we're all artists. In fact, maybe we all have an *obligation* to be artists because they have unique platforms from which they can create—their own perspectives. You're no different, even if you don't paint, sculpt, play the piano, wow the theater world with your thespian chops, or write novels.

3

You can be an artist when it comes to your career and your life, and I actually recommend approaching this first section devoted to "Creating Meaning" with an artist's heart—one that will allow you to sculpt your own unique personal and professional experience.

In your life, stand for something.

Domain: Meaning

Can you answer the question: *Who do I intend to be?*

Once you know who you intend to be, you can start to weigh your decisions and strategies against that knowledge. Before you can answer this question, consider the three "variables" below. These "variables" (values, strengths, self-awarness) are fundamental pieces of this larger question of who you intend to be.

Variables: Values, Strengths, Self-Awareness

Values: *What matters most to me?* (Variable 1)

We will all pursue the things that matter most to us. This can put you in a tough spot if your words don't match your actions. If you tell me that painting is what matters most to you, and you spend six hours a day watching TV and zero minutes painting, can you really say that you value painting more than TV? Your values will guide you, but your values are what you *do,* not what you say they are.

Strengths: *What is my superpower?* (Variable 2)

You are unique. There is no one else on earth, nor will there ever be, someone who has your exact thoughts, intentions, abilities, motivations, body, mind, and potential. This means that there are things you can do that no one else can. That means you have strengths, even if you downplay them or can't see their significance in the Big Picture. *Your* strengths will matter to others more than they might matter to you, and therefore you have an obligation to develop them to their potential.

Self-Awareness: *How do others see me, and how do I see myself?* (Variable 3)

We have beliefs about ourselves, and although those beliefs might appear static, the way we live in relation to them usually isn't. We tend to live up (or down) to our beliefs, similar to the way in which athletes may play better against a team they think is better than them, but may occasionally struggle to beat a team they should easily crush. Our beliefs are always running in the background, humming along, shaped by processes that we have not been (and may never be) completely aware of. They hold us in place, make us safe, offer certainty, and so on. But beliefs are *explored* territory. That's why they're safe. However, growth is not to be found in the domain of safety. If we really want to grow, we have to confront our beliefs—all of them. We have to see ourselves as we truly are, and often, it takes other people to act as our mirrors for us to see what's there.

The next three chapters are about "values," "strengths," and "self-awareness"—the variables that will help you answer the question of who you intend to be.

DOMAIN: MEANING
Variable 1 =
VALUES

- - - - - - - - - - - - - - - - - -

WHAT MATTERS MOST TO ME?

The main thing is to keep the main thing the main thing.

~ STEPHEN COVEY

What matters most to me?

Joe was an above-average business school undergraduate student, which was quite an accomplishment at the University of Michigan, the second-ranked program nationally. He was a diligent student who maintained his grades and had a polished look about him, which was characteristic of business school students.

When he handed me his resume, I smiled at the long list of activities that high-achieving students collect—president of a club, tons of volunteer experience, ran a marathon, high GPA. His list was long.

As his career advisor, I asked my first question: "So which industry are you looking to get into?"

"Finance." His response was quick and his tone flat.

"Do you like finance?" I prodded. Relaxing into my chair, I waited for the typical litany of reasons he thought finance would be great for him. Most students have this script practiced, as if they have spent some time talking themselves into it.

He shifted in his seat and looked down at the floor before answering. "I don't know if I like finance. I don't think I dislike it, but I don't know if I really like it."

Wow, what an intellectually honest answer, I thought to myself. *Most students have this ambivalence, but few students actually admit to it.*

Students are under tremendous pressure to "know what they want," so they pretend. They look at what is desirable to others and adopt that as their own.

At least this student is admitting that he doesn't know.

"You know, I had a classmate while at Columbia who was, prior to b-school, a ballerina. She would get all these phone calls from top consulting companies because they were intrigued by her background as a ballerina. One would think she'd be closing all these doors by becoming a ballerina, but this was not the case."

I paused and watched his expression soften.

"If you knew that you could still go into finance when you are an MBA, what would you do out of undergrad? What would be the most fun thing you could imagine?" I leaned forward onto the desk in front of me, smiling as I made eye contact.

He suddenly sat up a little straighter and said, "I want to train to be a chef. It would be fun to open a restaurant."

Now we're getting somewhere.

"That sounds fantastic…" and I started facilitating a conversation about how amazing life could be if he got to travel around to learn about and sample foods from different places. Then he could go and train to prepare the type of food which is an expression of who he is. Since he had a business undergrad training, he'd know enough to manage a fledgling business.

One of the hardest things about our twenties—or our college years in general—is that we're unsure of our identities.

Before college, before we're out on our own, whatever structure we had was largely dictated for us. In high school, you're part of a system and (hopefully) a stable home life where your peer groups and parents influence your identity. What amounts to you during those years is largely a product of who you're surrounded by. You can't just skip school and do your own thing. You can't defy your parents at every turn and expect harmony. You have choices, sure, but they're more limited than they'll be once you leave home.

In college, once you choose your classes and nail down your schedule, those structures that shaped your every waking moment back in high school vanish. Ironically, it's at this point of sudden independence when we can live however we want, that we realize that we don't know exactly who we are. The peer and family feedback that showed us who we were is gone. And that's where things get a little scary, because our identities are now unclear. Something in you wants to express itself, but what? How? What's the best way to live, now that no one is telling you how to do it?

This is the metaphorical crossroads. If you're like Joe, this is when you decide if you're going to crunch numbers because it seems like a sensible and reputable thing that you might do, or to become a chef, which your internal voice is whispering for you to do. It's the intersection of who you have been, butting up against who you might be. Now your job is to learn how to listen to the internal voice that's always running beneath the surface.

Your values are you, and you are your values.

What exactly is it that makes you "you?" What if you suddenly lost an arm, or a kidney, or a leg? Would you still be you? Of course. Your memories, your experiences, all of the days you have lived, and all of the events that have shaped you…they're all still there. You just weigh a little less and you'll have to adjust to life without that piece of your body.

Now let's say you kept your leg, arm, and kidney, but you no longer care about all of the things that used to be most important to you. Suddenly you care about things that are completely different. For instance, let's say you used to be a Jedi-level cheapskate who would have made Ebenezer Scrooge look altruistic, but now you're generous with your money. Or maybe you used to be a sports fanatic and now you think sports are an absolute waste of time. These whiplash shifts would be jarring to people who knew you, but would you still be the same person? Would you still be you?

Maybe not.

Imagine that you're in your favorite bookstore and that I'm the bookstore cat, lying on the counter, silently judging you and all of the browsers from my perch. For now, I'm going to focus on you and see if I can figure out who you are and what you value.

To start with, I'll watch where you go. Which section do you head to? Are you a reader of fiction? A history nut? A gardening enthusiast? A foodie with dreams of having a cooking show? A true crime buff who dabbles in amateur forensic studies? A philosophy major with unsolved theorems and axioms pushing you towards or away from some existential abyss?

As I watch you browse, I can infer what your values are with a reasonable degree of confidence. At the risk of sounding redundant, they are what you value. There is no clearer demonstration of this than the things we give our attention to, and the ways in which we spend our time. Strangely, even though this is obvious to me, the cat on the counter, it may not be obvious to you. Many of us never slow down enough to watch ourselves act, and to draw conclusions from our actions.

Back in human form, imagine that I sit you down, put you on the spot, and say, "Hey! What are your values? What do you really care about?" You might not be able to come up with a solid answer because the question asks you to do some real work.

After some time, you might say something like, "I value honesty," or, "I value religious faith." These things might sound and feel true to you. They might *be* true to you. But it's also important to know that our ideas about values can also get mixed up in what we think others value, or what society teaches us that we should care about.

For instance, think about what we might call "social ideals"—ideals that society insists we must *should* care about. "Financial responsibility," "American exceptionalism," "Integrity," "Liberty," "Free speech," and so on. Now, perhaps these are all great things, but saying that we value them is not equivalent to *actually* valuing them. If I watch you live your life for a week and your actions don't give me any clues about how important free speech, patriotism, and financial responsibility are to you, then I have the right to assume that they're not the things you value. However, when I see you online, planning a trip to Europe that you can't afford, despite your professed devotion to fiscal wisdom and frugality, I at least know that you *value* that trip to Europe.

Since direct questions rarely reveal the genuine answers, ask yourself some more indirect questions that might give some insight into what you value.

What kinds of books can I enjoy reading for hours?

What do I enjoy talking about in social settings?

What topics do I like to think about?

What dreams do I have about my future?

How do I spend most of my free time?

What do I spend money on?

These aren't abstractions. These questions have answers in your life.

In college, I didn't much care about my business classes. It might be more accurate to say that I found finance, marketing, and accounting lectures about as stimulating as an outhouse. So, I avoided those classes the way I might avoid an outhouse. Unsurprisingly, I didn't do well in those classes. But that didn't make me a terrible student across the board. In fact, I *always* went to German class, always did my work, and always put in every ounce of effort I could. Why?

Simple. I wasn't going to be a German professor or a Thomas Mann scholar who needed to read *The Magic Mountain* in its pure and pristine Teutonic glory, but when I was in high school I got to be an exchange student in Germany. A wonderful host family opened their doors to me and made me one of the family. Their English was as broken as my German, but we tried to communicate and were the better for it. When I got back to America, I vowed to become an exemplary student of

German. I wanted to go back to visit them, and be able to say and understand anything I wanted so I could get to know those wonderful people as well as possible.

That *mattered* to me, and my effort proved it. I can't say that my business classes mattered to me *at all,* and you need look no further than my inaction and apathy for evidence.

Looking at your choices can provide clues. Imagine that you have to choose between going to the library to study for an important final coming up in three days, or fulfilling an obligation you have to a dear sister to help her move. Or imagine that you've made a resolution to get to the gym this evening, but then your buddies call and invite you out for a raucous time. I'm not suggesting a moral element to either of these questions, but in each case, the choice you make is an indication of your priorities and values.

Let's now take a look at how we can make choices in our lives using our authentic values.

The most important choices are internal.

As a career counselor, I've spoken with a lot of students about their decisions. One of the most common conversations I have revolves around which college they should attend.

Should I attend School A or School B?

Do I take Class A or B? Profession A or B? Organization A or B?

These are *external* choices. To choose one means to choose something outside of yourself. They seem like big, significant choices. Committing to something that might take years seems like a big deal.

But there's another set of questions that are even more significant, and whose answers serve as better signposts. For instance:

> *Will I help my classmates in subject that I excel at?*
>
> *Will I change my diet so that I can have a healthier lifestyle?*
>
> *Will I help my sister move or get a jump on studying for finals?*
>
> *Will I start that podcast I've always thought about or not?*

These are all *internal* questions because the answer to each can only be derived from your values.

It's possible to change an external question into an internal question and thereby find a better, more useful answer. Instead of asking (an external question) "Which school should I go to?" you can ask an internal question, "What are the most important things for me to do while in school?" If you know the answer to the internal question, you'll probably find that you can get what you need from more than one school.

Rather than ask which profession to go into, consider instead: "How will I use my professional circumstances to serve a meaningful purpose?" If you can answer that question—which will require some hard thinking about personal meaning and purpose—you'll find that the professions you can use to bring about your goals aren't as limited as you might have thought.

I've known several people who, in private, tell me that they chose the wrong medical specialty, and yet, they're happy and fulfilled because they are able to engage in projects that they're passionate about. For these lucky people, it turned out that their happiness depended less on the formal choice of which medical specialization to commit to, and more on their inner resourcefulness to create professional opportunities. Because they have now asked (and answered) the internal questions, they can see their passions fulfilled despite having made what initially might have seemed like the "wrong" choice.

It's not that external questions and choices aren't important. They are, to an extent. Unfortunately, most people are seduced by external questions and choices, and fail to find meaning in their choices.

The most important questions and choices are internal.

Fulfillment comes from making choices consistent with your values.

Let's consider a previous example again. Should you go help your sister move, or should you get a jump on studying for that important final? There is not a "right" choice, meaning you couldn't show a group of scientists the choice between helping your sister move and studying for a final and get empirical consensus. But there's a right choice for *you*, and that right choice is the one that aligns with your values.

Disclaimer: There are some exceptions, but they venture into the realm of pathology. You are not making a "right" choice if your values require you to hinder others' ability to choose. There's also a difference between hurting someone and inconveniencing them, or even disappointing them. You can make the right choice for you and still have people judge your choice unfavorably, but that's on them.

You should go help your sister move because that's what a good sibling does, right? But wait, you should go to the library to study because you have a commitment to being an excellent student, right?

Unfortunately, life is a balancing act of prioritization that never stops and is rarely easy. For now, it's deciding whether to help your sister move or be more prepared for your final. Later on, it's whether you should go to Johnny's recital or stay late at work to finish an important report for work.

These choices will always be coming at you.

I'm convinced that it's wisest to start with values when making decisions. This is why I insist that the people who come to me for help in making decisions start by asking themselves the internal questions that will help them plot a course. When you prioritize according to your values, all the important stuff that you care about gets done. That's the takeaway here.

When you're eighty-five years old and looking back at your life, your definition of success might be different than the one you have today, but it doesn't have to be. You get to decide how you will measure your life. With proper planning, all of the important things will get done. The more frequently you see that you can create the results you want, the more excited you'll get about looking inside yourself to make sure that your values continue to align with your actions.

It's hard for me not to picture an eighty-five-year-old version of Joe, the student who arrived at the crossroads of spreadsheets and traveling the world as a chef. I don't know if he went on to be a banker or a chef; but based on what he told me, I know what I hope he's doing.

> **Key Lesson:** *Know what is important.*
>
> **Key Points:**
> - *Your values are you, and you are your values.*
> - *The most important choices are internal.*
> - *Fulfillment comes from making choices consistent with your values.*

Action Steps for Learning

Action 1: Inventory Your Actions and Preferences

What do we consider important? No matter what we say, our actions are a strong indicator of our values. Ask yourself the questions below. Identify some themes from your answers. They are likely to be indicators of your values.

What kinds of books can I enjoy reading for hours?

What do I enjoy talking about in social settings?

What topics do I like to think about?

What dreams do I have about my future?

How do I spend most of my free time?

What do I spend money on?

Action 2: Pick Your "Value Words"

Go to the worksheet called "Value Words" later in this chapter. Review the words on that page and circle the three to five words which you feel most represents the type of person that you are.

Action 3: Highs and Lows

Think of three instances in your life where you were the most proud of yourself. What were the values that you were expressing during those instances? Think of three instances in your life where you were the most dissatisfied with yourself. What were the values that were being suppressed during those instances?

Notes on Other Actions

What other actions could you take?

Worksheet: Life Wheel

In the wheel below, circle a number which indicates how important that domain of life is for you. Assign a number from 1 to 5, where *5 = most important* and where *1 = least important*.

Keep in mind:

- Multiple domains can have the same number (e.g. career and social can both have a "5" or a "1").

- The total of all the numbers in the 8 domains may not exceed 25.

- *The number for each domain is based on what you WANT, rather than the current state for how you allocate your energy now.*

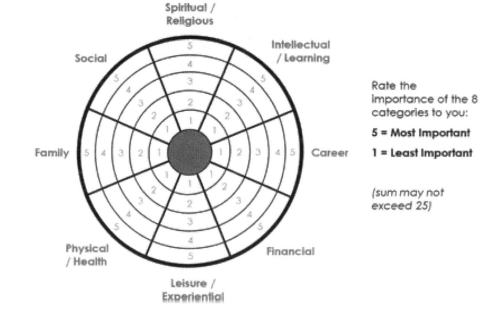

Now, force rank the 8 domains from 1 (most important) to 8 (least important). **Note:** *This ranking may change over the course of your life. These are not static but reflective of where you are now.*

1.   5.

2.   6.

3.   7.

4.   8.

Worksheet: Value Words[1]

Accountability	Discretion	Humility	Rigor
Accuracy	Diversity	Inclusivity	Security
Achievement	Dynamism	Independence	Self-actualization
Adventurousness	Economy	Ingenuity	Self-control
Altruism	Effectiveness	Inner Harmony	Selflessness
Ambition	Efficiency	Inquisitiveness	Self-reliance
Assertiveness	Elegance	Insightfulness	Sensitivity
Balance	Empathy	Intelligence	Serenity
Being the best	Enjoyment	Intellectual Status	Service
Belonging	Enthusiasm	Intuition	Shrewdness
Boldness	Equality	Joy	Simplicity
Calmness	Excellence	Justice	Soundness
Carefulness	Excitement	Leadership	Speed
Challenge	Expertise	Legacy	Spontaneity
Cheerfulness	Exploration	Love	Stability
Clear-mindedness	Expressiveness	Loyalty	Strategic
Commitment	Fairness	Making a difference	Strength
Community	Faith	Mastery	Structure
Compassion	Family-orientedness	Merit	Success
Competitiveness	Fidelity	Obedience	Support
Consistency	Fitness	Openness	Teamwork
Contentment	Fluency	Order	Temperance
Continuous Improvement	Focus	Originality	Thankfulness
Contribution	Freedom	Patriotism	Thoroughness
Control	Fun	Perfection	Thoughtfulness
Cooperation	Generosity	Piety	Timeliness
Correctness	Goodness	Positivity	Tolerance
Courtesy	Grace	Practicality	Traditionalism
Creativity	Growth	Preparedness	Trustworthiness
Curiosity	Happiness	Professionalism	Truth-seeking
Decisiveness	Hard Work	Prudence	Understanding
Dependability	Health	Quality-orientation	Uniqueness
Determination	Helping Society	Reliability	Unity

---

1   Word list from Mind Tools.com (https://www.mindtools.com/pages/article/new TED_85.htm)

Word Problems: Values = ?

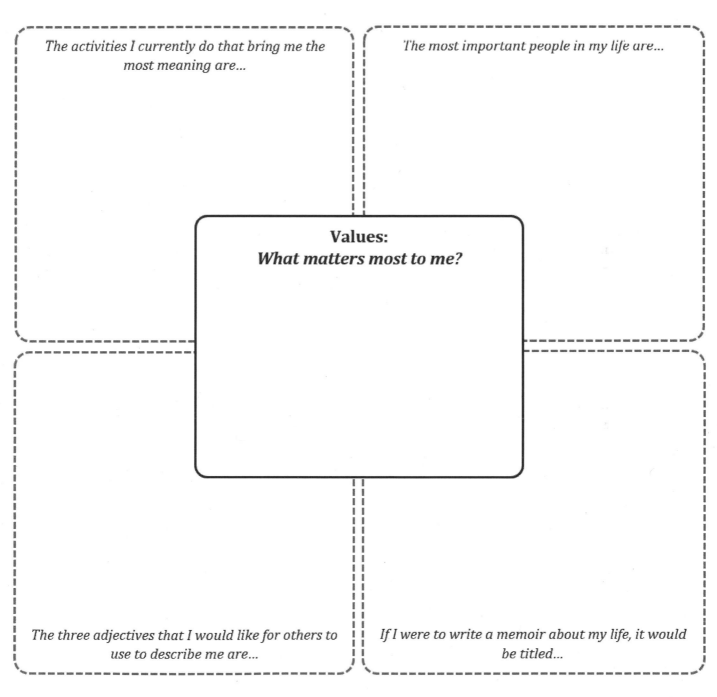

The activities I currently do that bring me the most meaning are...

The most important people in my life are...

Values:
What matters most to me?

The three adjectives that I would like for others to use to describe me are...

If I were to write a memoir about my life, it would be titled...

DOMAIN: MEANING

Variable 2 =
STRENGTHS

- - - - - - - - - - - - - - - - - - -

WHAT IS MY SUPERPOWER?

*Strengths are not activities you're good at,
they're activities that strengthen you. A strength
is an activity that before you're doing it, you look
forward to doing it; while you're doing it, time
goes by quickly and you can concentrate; after
you've done it, it seems to fulfill a need of yours.*

~ MARCUS BUCKINGHAM

What is my superpower?

Kate, a young woman in her mid-twenties with a carefree air, sat across from me in the university cafeteria. "I'm not sure I'm a very good student. I mean, I'm not a *bad* student, but I wouldn't say that I'm that great as a student either."

Kate was a second-year medical student with a quick wit. She always had the right joke to lighten up a situation. I occasionally checked in with her to see how she and her classmates were responding to the challenges of medical school, and she had mentioned that she'd like to chat with me over lunch.

"Well, I guess it depends on what you mean by *good* student," I prompted.

"I'm definitely not at the top of the class grade-wise. I think I'm doing well, but my grades are closer towards the middle of the class than the top." She poked at her food, obviously unhappy about the facts.

This young lady has no idea what her superpowers are, I thought as I watched her push the food around on her plate.

"I do have to tell you something," she continued. "Last week, after I did a workshop with a few first-year med students about setting personal goals, I had so many students wanting to talk to me for advice. I was telling Jack (a school academic advisor) and he said that he wasn't surprised. He said that I am a 'people magnet.'"

"That is a great description!" I enthusiastically affirmed. "I have noticed that you can really cheer people up with your positivity and humor, and then people are drawn to you. If you were a superhero, that would probably be your superpower."

We had a laugh about that, but there was no denying that Kate really did have this rather amazing gift.

I didn't want her to leave this lunch without understanding how much of a strength this actually was for her, so I continued. "In your class of stressed-out med students, you are probably at the top of your class in terms of 'people magnetism.' They really do rely on you to provide that lightness that you bring. When you become a resident, you will more likely be the top person in 'people magnetism' again. When you are a practicing doctor, you are likely to be the top 'people magnet' in your group. When you're thirty-five, who's going to care about grades? What will matter then?" I coaxed.

Kate's shoulders went back and she gave me the biggest smile I'd seen from her. I could see that she was beginning to own her true strength—one that reflected who she was and would stay with and serve her for the rest of her life if she would just understand it and never let it go.

What a shame that schools often promote grades as the standard, when excellence also resides in everyone through the exercise of their unique strengths, I thought as we finished the last few bites of our lunch.

"Okay, go and use your superpower for justice and good!" I cheered as I stood up to leave.

"I will!" she exclaimed and promptly flexed her arms to show me she had really grasped all of this superpower talk.

If you're like most people, you probably spend more time in school or at work than you do at home. And this means that you probably spend more time with your classmates or coworkers than with your family. At least you love your job (or studies), right? Right? Well, while I'm waiting for your answer, here's a monumentally depressing statistic: According to a Gallup poll, over seventy percent of Americans "hate their stupid jobs."

How is that even possible? The answer is simple, even if it's not intuitive: Most people don't know what their strengths are. Peter Drucker said:[3]

> *Most Americans do not know what their strengths are. When you ask them, they look at you with a blank stare, or they respond in terms of subject knowledge, which is the wrong answer.*

Do you believe Drucker? Can you conceive of a reality where people truly don't know their own strengths? How is that even possible?

We're not wired to see "strengths."

Imagine that your son or daughter has just gotten a report card. You look it over and here's what you see:

Where does your attention go? Be honest.

You're not looking at that A+ in Art. No, unless you're a rare bird indeed, you're looking at that C in Science, perhaps lamenting a future in which your child does not win a Nobel Prize for anything scientific.

Why do we do that?

Let's leave the report card behind for a moment and go for a walk in the woods. After a few minutes of walking and thinking, you step into a clearing where you are greeted by three objects:

Which one of this odd triad are you focused on?

The bear, of course! And if you think the apple looks tastier than the bear looks dangerous, watch the bear attack scene in "The Revenant" and your priorities will realign themselves.

These examples all fall under the umbrella of what scientists call "negativity bias."[4] Any version of negativity bias can be described as, "Your brain tries to keep you alive by pointing out potential dangers." Those dangers are most obviously manifest in things that are different—things that announce themselves. Thankfully, you don't need a Gallup poll to know that we're being chased by bears less than ever, and yet the negativity bias creeps into everything.

Now, let's backtrack a bit, all the way to caveman days. Imagine that you're in a cave, sitting around a fire with your tribe mates.

Which face holds your attention?

Can you really afford to fixate on the smiles when someone is glaring at you with obvious hostility? No. When someone is angry with you, then and now, that actually represents an existential threat for you within the structure of your little group. Our attention gives priority to negativity and danger, elevating them so that we can't help but notice them…and protect ourselves as necessary.

Think about the healthcare industry. Almost twenty percent of the US GDP goes to it. Ask yourself what the goal of the healthcare industry is. Would you guess that it's more focused on "treating sickness" or "promoting health"?

This is a rhetorical question. Nearly all of the money goes to treating sickness. Well, knowing that, how healthy is our current society? Can we achieve optimal levels of health in the U.S. with a sole focus on sickness?

Society, just like individual people, trends towards what we can call a "broken frame." We're always trying to fix things that are bad and/or broken. We spend less time thinking about how to make things good, better, or good and better to the point that things don't break as often to begin with.

Now, back to the report card.

You can now see one reason why we are drawn to notice the negative over the positive. This can apply to things outside of evolutionary and societal adaptations, as well. If you hear ten nice things about yourself, and then you hear one truly biting, hateful comment, which are you most likely to focus on? The fact that there were more pleasantries than barbs has nothing to do with the mode that your attention rushes towards. In that instance, it's not about survival, but your system still goes on alert.

With all of this focus on the "negativity" and "brokenness" and "potential danger," it's easy to see why most people are generally unaware of their strengths…and more likely to be painfully aware of their flaws.

So we shouldn't just focus on flaws. Remember magnetic Kate? By focusing on the areas where she didn't excel, she overlooked the part of her which was her true source of excellence.

Your strengths are the "real" you.

You can protest all you want, but you have gifts. We all do. We all have a "superpower" that no one else does. Maybe our superpowers wouldn't make it into a blockbuster Marvel adaptation, but that doesn't mean that they aren't there. It's a bittersweet irony that it's through the exercise of unique strengths that each of us can figure out who we really are, and who we could be. But you can't exercise strengths that you don't know exist.

If an alien race were studying us all as children to predict which of us would become Army officers, I might have invalidated all of their hypotheses. The Army brochures and commercials don't say, "Bring us your nerdy, reserved, humanists who love to study philosophy for fun. Also, make sure they're slower than the other kids, of mediocre marksmanship, and the opposite of John Wayne."

However, I *was* known as the "man with the plan."I had a knack for knowing what to do next in whatever situation I found myself stuck. Maybe not like Jack Bauer in "24," but a knockoff version. Lost in the dark with my unit in the woods? No problem. Here are steps 1 to 8 to extricate ourselves. Need to move 100 vehicles from point A to point B with minimal advanced warning? No problem. Need to create a defensive perimeter for the company while being short 30% of personnel? No problem. I already had a plan. I just had it. I could "see" what needed to be done.

It didn't take a lot of effort on my part, but we all benefited from it. That's what you want in an officer, but I couldn't have known it without being in the situation. Today, I'm not in the Army anymore, but I'm still that "man with the plan." I'm still giving advice to people in complex situations. It's how I help. And while I've gotten better at it with practice, the essential gift has been there all along. It was always a strength.

The clinical psychologist Jordan B. Peterson has a wonderful program called Self Authoring.[5] Essentially, it's a writing program that allows people to create their own biography, along with a plan for the future. He describes its core purpose as a plan to help people "justify their own existence." That might sound harsh, but it's not intended to be. As a professor at the University of Toronto, Peterson realized, with ever-growing horror, that most students had never been made to sit down, think about what they wanted, and plan for it. He doesn't imply that students have no Big Picture reason to exist but that, unless they are pursuing their own vision, tailored to their own strengths, with dogged determination, they will forever fall short of who they could have been.

Our education system falls woefully, wretchedly short in this regard. Many universities are mere middle-management factories whose purpose could not be more distant from helping students discover their own gifts. Perhaps it's too much to expect that a university guide you towards what you might do, but it definitely should guide you towards knowing what you might do better than others.

Ugh, that report card. Grading period after grading period, that pesky C in Science refuses to budge. The A+ in Art is just as stubborn. If you had to put money on it, is the child more likely to become a scientist or an author? An author, of course. Now, what might we do with that information?

It takes far less energy to move from first-rate performance to excellence than it does to move from incompetence to mediocrity. ~ Peter Drucker

Want to guarantee mediocrity? Then focus primarily on fixing weaknesses. How much benefit does the world get if we insist that C students in Science see it through and become passable scientists? Is that what we want from our scientists, doctors, authors, and artists—good enough? Ask yourself that the next time you're on an operating table and you can choose between the C and the A+ student. Chances are, the surgeon with the A+ showed the aptitude for meticulous, high-stakes work all along.

You and I are suited for different things, and our differing interests, passions, fears, histories, ages, experiences, psychological traits, and even geographies work together to signal the roles that we should probably be playing. Part of education is, or should be, a question of helping people know their roles. And I'm not talking about any sort of guild system where, because

I was a blacksmith, my son can never aspire to be more than a blacksmith despite his occupational aspirations. Roles, in this instance, are interchangeable with what I'm calling gifts.

In a large Gallup study on human strengths, Donald Clifton, Marcus Buckingham, and Tom Rath found that:[6]

> *People who indicate that they have the opportunity to focus on their strengths are six times more likely to be engaged in their jobs and three times more likely to report having an excellent quality of life in general.*

Not surprising.

Imagine that I'm working at a cash register at a department store. I have a clear set of tasks and duties. If you, despite any differences between us, can perform those duties equally well, then each of us is replaceable with respect to that job. This applies to any role from cashier to neurosurgeon. If you define yourself based on a set of external criteria, you are replaceable.

Do you want to be irreplaceable? Then you must figure out what your (unique) strengths are, not just the things that you're capable of doing.

Now, if you're buying into this and you don't feel like you know what your strengths are, here are some questions to ponder:

What activities am I naturally interested in? (These are not "entertainment" activities, but ones which require you to "show up" and apply yourself).

What seems to come easily and naturally to me?

What role do I find myself playing within a team?

What am I the "go to" person for?

Spend some time looking at the activities below. Which activities do you find most compelling? (Circle three to five activities which is more natural to you)[7]

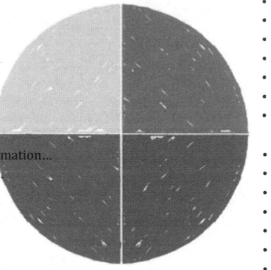

- Form a coalition...
- Develop a community...
- Teach and educate...
- Support and develop...
- Promote a culture...
- Empower a group...
- Build awareness...

- Gather and provide information...
- Analyze data for insight...
- Develop measurement...
- Standardize a process...
- Organize a system...
- Develop policy...
- Manage a complex effort...

- Discover a new method...
- Design a new product...
- Found an organization...
- Transform existing methods...
- Create a new program...
- Open a new practice...
- Experiment...

- Run an organization...
- Achieve goals...
- Enable decision...
- Initiate action...
- Respond to crises/challenge...
- Implement a policy...
- Orchestrate a campaign...

Here are additional resources to further explore your strengths:

- **VIA Character Strengths Survey:**

  http://www.viacharacter.org/www/Character-Strengths-Survey

- **Strengthsfinder 2.0**

  http://strengths.gallup.com/110440/About-StrengthsFinder-20.aspx

- **Superpower Cards by SY Partners**

  https://superpowers.sypartners.com/

- **Reflected Best Self Exercise**

  http://positiveorgs.bus.umich.edu/cpo-tools/reflected-best-self-exercise-2nd-edition/

Maximize the contribution of your unique gifts.

Want to know the most poorly kept secret in the world? Consumption—getting stuff—doesn't lead to happiness, but Contribution does. We've been duped, sometimes willingly, and sometimes by sophisticated teams of marketing experts, website engineers, and unscrupulous masters of persuasion. You see, consumption is passive. It goes nowhere. It produces nothing. It doesn't require you to be a part of it. If you turn your TV on and walk around the block, the TV is still doing what it does. It and the products it displays don't need you. They don't know you exist. They don't require you to contribute.

Why does that matter? Because research is beginning to show us that instead of Consumption, Contribution is what we want.[8]

Contribution makes us want to get up in the morning. It requires us to engage, connect with people, and create the best versions of ourselves so that we can all improve…together. And if we're all in the right roles—right for each one of us—it can only lead to the best possible outcome for society.

Nothing will give you greater satisfaction than knowing how to maximize your contribution. Tomorrow, I could probably go work at McDonald's or I could go mow lawns. Those are both contributions of a sort. However, the question is, "What is the highest level of contribution I am capable of?"

The greater your level of contribution (i.e. the more value you provide), the more you will receive.

For a time, I was a financial analyst, making a type of contribution that required a certain level of knowledge and skill. However, it didn't utilize my main strengths of creativity and empathy. Therefore, staying in finance, although it was a good-paying job, would not have allowed me to maximize what I am capable of contributing because it did not tap into my natural talents. So, I decided to leave finance.

My next job was in career advising. That job did utilize more of my talents. It was fun and at the end of three years, I was able to create my next job at the medical school just based on my confidence and reputation. Ever since then, I have been able to create my own jobs, meaning that I would not apply for a job role, but I would look at an organization, see what they needed, and propose a job based on my talents and how those would translate to solving their problems.

There's a saying that goes, "You can measure the size of a person by the size of the person's problems." As you advance in your learning and in your career, the hope is that the size of the problems that you are capable of handling grows. Don't think of it as applying for ever-higher job titles. Instead, think of it as handling an ever-higher level of challenge, which is another way of saying that you will contribute more.

How will you handle higher levels of challenge? What is the highest level of challenge that you can handle?

> The highest level of challenge you can handle is aligned with the highest development of your natural talents.

Kate and I had many chances to talk about medical school after our initial talk about her superpowers. I always asked her, "How are you doing with med school?" Almost always, she would answer, "I'm doing GREAT!" Sometimes, she would even tell me she surprised herself with how well she was doing. (After all, med school is known for a certain degree of miserable grind.) Part of what kept her going, she reflected during one of our chats, was her connection with herself and her superpower: "Once I knew who I am, that took away so much of the fear and anxiety about myself and not being good enough."

You will realize that once you have developed your natural talents to a sufficient degree, there is no job description that will fully capture what you are capable of doing. You will be a unique contributor. Instead of having to apply for jobs with generic job descriptions because you were generic and had to pursue job opportunities, you will be able to create jobs that solve problems and make you excited to go to work every day.

If someone wants what you have, they will have to come to you. You will be indispensable. The tables will have turned. Now the opportunities will pursue you!

You'll also gain a certain level of mastery. When you're a master at something, your strengths are no longer a mere category—they're an expression of what makes you unique. At that point, you're in a position to give to others from your maximum potential. Few things will fill you with as much joy as giving to people to whom you have become indispensable.

That's how I view effective education: Every educator's purpose is to help students figure out their unique contribution, and then to help them gain whatever tools they need to nurture, grow, and master their gifts.

The meaning of life is to find your gift. The purpose of life is to give it away.
~ Pablo Picasso

Key Lesson: *Apply your talents.*

Key Points:
- *We're not wired to see "strengths."*
- *Your strengths are the "real" you.*
- *Maximize the contribution of your unique gifts.*

Action Steps for Learning

Action 1: Teach on a Topic

What is a skill you are trying to develop some expertise around? Sure, you can take class or a workshop on that topic. Or… how about volunteering to teach on that topic? Often, teaching is a more effective way to learn. You don't need to be a PhD on that topic to be able to teach others. You just need to be better than those you are teaching. Look for opportunities to teach.

Action 2: Read for Depth

According to the Pew Research Center, 24% of U.S. adults did not read a single book in 2017. If you want to develop an exceptional level of knowledge on a topic, you will need to focus your reading efforts. What if you read ten books on a topic of your interest in the next twelve months? Before long, you will be the expert on that topic.

Action 3: Find Opportunities to Practice

How long does it take to be okay at something? Not as long as you think. If you've never played the guitar before, but practiced for twenty hours, you'd actually be passable. To get to twenty hours, it's better to do twenty minutes a day for sixty days. The secret is not to try to do ten hours of practice one day and then give up. Keep chipping away little by little. You can become a master at just about anything with sustained practice.

Notes on Other Actions

What other actions could you take?

Word Problems: Strengths = ?

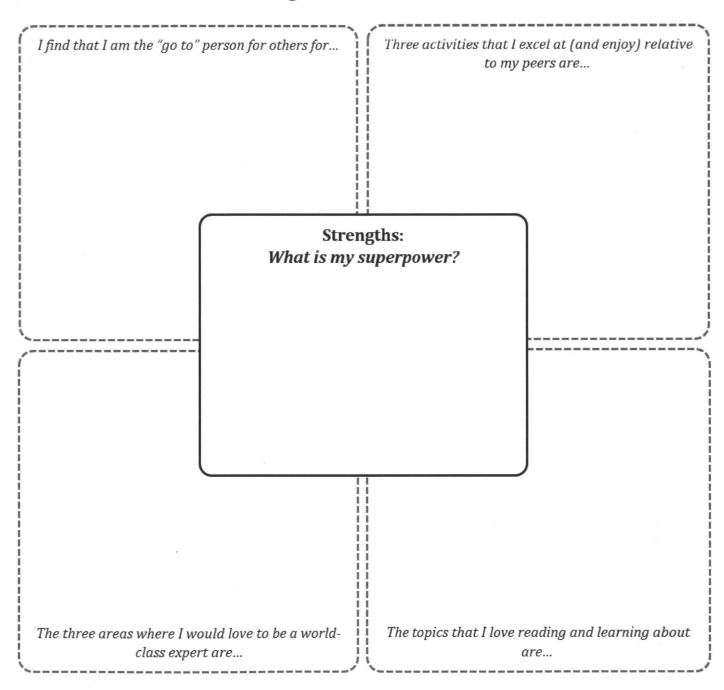

I find that I am the "go to" person for others for…

Three activities that I excel at (and enjoy) relative to my peers are…

Strengths:
What is my superpower?

The three areas where I would love to be a world-class expert are…

The topics that I love reading and learning about are…

DOMAIN: MEANING

Variable 3 =
SELF-AWARENESS

- - - - - - - - - - - - - - -

HOW DO OTHERS SEE ME, AND HOW DO I SEE MYSELF?

*Until you make the unconscious conscious, it
will direct your life and you will call it fate.*

~ CARL JUNG

How do others see me, and how do I see myself?

Claire, a junior faculty member at the medical school, walked into my office and dropped herself somewhat dramatically into the chair across from my desk. "I have to meet with the chair of my department to negotiate for my salary soon." The statement was accompanied by an eye roll.

I always enjoy her visits, I thought as I sat back in my chair and responded. "I'm assuming, from your eye roll, that you're not looking forward to this?"

"Correcto. I hate these things." She shifted herself to a more comfortable position in the chair.

"What? I thought you became a doctor in order to experience the joy of negotiation!" I thought a little sarcasm would help her relax a little more.

She smirked. "I don't think that I'm necessarily better than the other faculty in the department. It'll be hard to make the case that I deserve a bump in salary," she mused, still appearing deflated.

"Well that may be the story that you are telling yourself, but I think you've accomplished a great deal in the last two years that deserves recognition, and not just an 'atta, girl!' Didn't you secure that major grant for diabetes research? Didn't you get invited to give a couple of major talks at your key national meetings? Didn't you get the award for the most 'coolly decorated office' at the holiday party?"

It's hard to believe she doesn't see how successful she's been.

"Yeah, you know, I do need to do a better job at looking at myself. I'm actually pretty kick-ass if you look at it 'objectively.'" A wry smile spread across her young face.

We spent the next half hour discussing negotiation strategies, identifying areas of strength that she could use to make a stronger case for herself.

"Tony, thanks for helping me think through this process. I feel much better than I did half an hour ago—about myself, the work that I do, and the possibility of this raise. Still, I'm a little bit scared. I wish I had a bit more confidence."

"Okay. Let me ask you, what is the most important thing in your life?" I asked.

"My family. I have two small daughters and they are the center of my life. I'm always trying to be a good role model for them," she answered quickly.

"Then when you're negotiating, can you also be negotiating for the world that you want your daughters to enter?" I wondered.

"YES! That's something I can negotiate for with full confidence!" She beamed and just about bounced out of the office.

Atta, Girl! I smiled as I jumped back into the pile of papers on my desk.

Because our narratives influence our confidence and expectations, they drive our lives, choices, and experiences even when we are not thinking about them.

We get what we expect. This truth spans academic disciplines, self-improvement books, career trajectories, and just about every other adventure that's driven by the stories we tell ourselves.

There's some research about maids that can clue us in here. Yes, I said maids.

Our lives are driven by our narratives.

If you've stayed in a few hotels, you've probably encountered a few maids. Think about their jobs. When you start dividing it up into tasks, those maids spend nearly every minute of their shifts engaged in physical labor. Lugging, lifting, scrubbing, pulling, pushing, stooping, mopping, and more. And yet, a study revealed that 67% of maids reported that they did no exercise. No exercise at all! Why would they think this? [9]

Because of their perception that "exercise" is something like an hour on a treadmill.

Ellen Langer, the study's author, set out to see if she could change their perceptions.

Eighty-four maids had agreed to participate in the study. To start with, she and her team took the measurements generally considered to represent the state of a person's health: body fat, waist-to-hip ratio, blood pressure, weight, and body mass index.

After dividing them into two groups, the study began. With one group, the maids gave a thorough inventory of their daily tasks and then Langer told them that the physical activity of their job already meant they were meeting the Surgeon General's benchmarks for an active lifestyle.

She didn't tell the other group anything.

After one month, Langer and her team performed the tests on the group that had been told they were already active and, essentially, exercising. After going through the physical measurements again, the results were astonishing. The women who had been told they were already exercising enough experienced significant drops in blood pressure, weight, and hip-to-waist ratio. This wasn't because they had started exercising. This was the result of them starting to see that they already were exercising.

Our mindsets and narratives matter.

Growing up, my parents told me I was good at math. My teachers told me the same thing, and so did my classmates and friends. Can you guess why? (Hint: because I was Asian.) At the time, I didn't have any reason to question them. I did seem to be good at math. Today, with the perspective of time, I can see that I had no intrinsic advantage in math. I didn't even like it. I was a regular guy with brains, but no salient mathematical aptitude. I just lived up to what everyone told me: "You're good at math." Well, if everyone was saying it, it seemed like it was my job to make sure that they weren't wrong. They put me in a category and I ran with it.

Our lives are made of expectations and beliefs just like these that shift, vanish, mutate, and strengthen with age and (hopefully) wisdom. When you were young, you were just a little lump moving through a gigantic, uncertain world. You couldn't think about how vast it all was because you had no sense of life's complications. And yet, those exploratory years are nothing but learning.

That stove is hot. I know because I touched it.

When I cry, someone will come and take care of me. I know because that's what happens.

I wonder what will happen if I push over that tower of blocks? Ah, a pleasant crash and the thrill of seeing my parents pick them up after they scatter across the floor.

My parents are fighting. I wonder if that's because of me? It must be, because all I think about—all I am really capable of thinking about at this point—is me.

This question and response pattern is how all learning works. When we get older, it just gets more specific and task-oriented. Will I have enough food? Will I have enough money? Am I smart enough? How good-looking am I? Do people like me? Should I be, or try to be, more social?

But being an adult in no way guarantees that the answers to these questions are accurate, because the answers are based on beliefs, insecurities, and narratives that were developed when they were young. Having millions of dollars doesn't guarantee that people are happy, and it doesn't guarantee that they'll stop trying to earn even more. The sense of financial insecurity doesn't necessarily evaporate with wealth. Trying to figure out if you're smart enough can be a minefield for self-esteem, because good luck getting a consensus on what smart, educated, and intelligent even means. And being a likable person is dependent on how other people see and react to you.

The author Martha Beck makes an important distinction between "clean" pain and "dirty" pain.[10] Clean pain is not making a sports team that you had really wanted to make. Bummer. The pain is just from the disappointment of that occurrence. Dirty pain is saying, "I knew I was never going to make the team! This type of thing always happens to me! Sports is a waste of my time anyway!"

One type of pain comes from reality but the other comes from a story that serves no one and helps nothing. In a way, the stories you tell yourself about your reality *are* your reality.

If you're going to grow, you have to believe and expect that you can grow. That requires stories about growth. And those stories have to be challenging, because growth is a challenge. Self-awareness is a challenge. It's an acknowledgment that the

SOLVING FOR "WHY" | ANTONIUS TSAI

narratives that used to protect you may need to be set aside, in the way that a young crab must shed the shell that once kept it safe and look for a bigger one.

Unless you expect things to be different, how would they be most likely to change?

When I worked in corporate finance, I had a good job with a salary that took care of everything I needed. But it didn't take long for me to leave the corporate world to go into education, and take the 50% pay cut in the process. I was willing to take the cut because I thought that I would be more fulfilled in the education field. Not making as much was just the price of working in education. At least, that's what I expected.

But when I reflected on my situation, I found some holes in my thinking. It was kind of like feeling like your back is against the wall and then realizing there's not even a wall there. I had just assumed that since I was working in education, my income *must* be less. I told myself, "I'm an idealist! I don't care about money." All that just served to reinforce my reality that I wasn't making that much money despite my contribution.

What was another way to view the situation?

I had a versatile degree and a skillset that could lend itself to many different structures. Maybe I could use what I had learned to make the amount of money I wanted, in the field I wanted. *I had to give myself permission to make more money.* It wasn't that other people weren't willing to pay me for my value. It was my job to acknowledge and own my value, and realize that I could be paid well regardless of the field I worked in.

I resolved to double my salary. Long story short, I didn't revolutionize the education field to the point where the salary cap rose sky-high and everyone including me got bumped up to double the pay grade; but I took actions that would make it more likely for me to make more money. Shortly after I made this shift in my narrative, a new position opened up unexpectedly and made it possible for me to double my salary without heading back to Corporate Land.

These kinds of stories can start to feel a little woo-woo, but don't worry, this isn't about the "Law" of Attraction or rushing out to buy a copy of *The Secret*. I just want you to see that I had to first change my internal expectations in order to realize the changes that I wanted for my outer circumstances. I imagined what the scene of my victory would be and I got myself there through actions.

Can you imagine the scene of your victory? What will it look like when you have arrived? You'll want to be able to answer this question, so you can recognize your success when you have it.

Now, for the narrative that needs some shifting.

When you picture the "scene of your victory", you'll also feel some resistance to it. *What is the resistance inside of you*? What's the internal monologue like? How exactly does your fear try to convince you that it isn't possible or feasible, and that you're impossibly naïve? What words does it use? What does your resistance say about what you expect from your own story?

> *Your brain is like a supercomputer, and your self-talk is the program it will run.*
> ~ Jim Kwik

When you begin to adjust your narrative and open up to the possibilities that are already there, amazing things can happen.

A few months after our meeting, I had a chance to reconnect with Claire.

"So how did it go?" I asked her.

"It was still scary, but I made sure to remind myself that this negotiation was not just about getting more money. It was about so much more than that. I made sure not to lose that perspective during the negotiation. There were a few key moments where it felt like a staring contest. Wow, that was a lot of pressure! But I kept going back to my 'why' for this negotiation. In the end, it was *he* who blinked first! It was like I passed a test, and after that, we negotiated on more 'equal' terms. I didn't get everything I wanted, but I got a lot of it. I think he felt good with it too…strange. This didn't feel like just another negotiation. It felt like I negotiated with myself for permission to own my power. It *meant* so much more to me."

That's what's possible when you intentionally direct your internal narrative.

We can make our own meaning.

There's a parable about three stonecutters. Each of them is working the stone with hammers and chisels. A man asks each of them what they are doing. The first stonecutter says, "I'm cutting stones." The second says, "I'm making a living." The third says, "I'm building a cathedral."

They're all performing the same actions, but the action's meanings are different to each person. Each stonecutter has a different story about what he's doing, and the same action is, respectively, a job, a career, and a calling. On the continuum of good, better, and best, which stonecutter has the best perspective? The more meaning we can attribute to our actions, the more fulfilled we will be. And this is true even for happy people. Who would turn down the chance to be even a little bit happier, and why would we do that?

Have you ever experienced a situation one way and then another, almost completely opposite way in hindsight?

An example. My mom was on a trip to Asia when her basement flooded. Her water heater had been leaking and made her the proud owner of a downstairs swamp. We didn't clap our hands and exclaim about our good fortune, but there were positives about the experience. One of her neighbors went above and beyond helping her make things right, and the bond they formed as a result is precious to them both. It also gave my mom a chance to get rid of a lot of things she no longer needed. And when the insurance money came through, she got $17,000.

Since my house burned down
I now have a better view
Of the rising moon

~ Masahide

Every experience that initially looks like a failure, a disappointment, or an annoyance, can actually be framed in the positive. Imagine that you didn't get a job, or that you flunked a test. Or maybe you got dumped by your boyfriend or girlfriend. These all look and feel terrible on the surface, but none of them are objectively bad. And yet, you can certainly tell yourself a story that will convince you that they're bad.

But what if, instead, you said, "Thank heavens I didn't get that job, because a better one is coming." Or what if you told yourself that you lost that relationship because the right person for you is still out there. And even if failing a test momentarily hinders your academic momentum, if it leads to you studying harder, it's still a net positive when you weigh the results in the long run.

You control the meaning you give to things in your life.

Think about the resistance that I asked you to consider before. *What is the resistance inside of you?* Think about them from a narrative view that doesn't serve you.

Example: *People don't understand me.*

Now ask yourself if that's really true. Then, try shifting the narrative to something more like this: It's not peoples' job to understand me. They're just going about their lives. I can communicate my wants and needs, so if I feel misunderstood, there must be more to it.

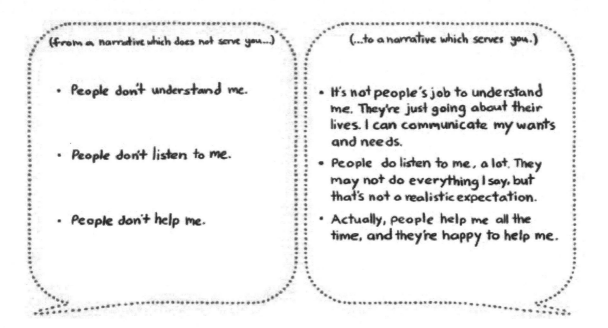

(from a narrative which does not serve you...)

- People don't understand me.

- People don't listen to me.

- People don't help me.

(...to a narrative which serves you.)

- It's not people's job to understand me. They're just going about their lives. I can communicate my wants and needs.
- People do listen to me, a lot. They may not do everything I say, but that's not a realistic expectation.
- Actually, people help me all the time, and they're happy to help me.

Try doing this with every limiting belief you can identify. For every limiting narrative you have rattling in your head, replace that narrative with one that serves you. For example, you may say to yourself, "People don't help me." Again, is that true? While it may be true that not everyone helps you all the time in the way that you want, people likely do help you. It is your narrative that filters that true fact of your story out and makes you believe that it's not true.

I think you'll be surprised at how easy it is to prove yourself wrong, or at least show yourself where there might be more to the story than you have previously admitted or realized.

We must learn to shape our inner worlds in this way before we can successfully tell ourselves and experience new stories.

When we are no longer able to change a situation, we are challenged to change ourselves. ~ Viktor Frankl

If you're unfamiliar with Victor Frankl, he was a Jewish man who survived as a prisoner of Nazi Germany's death camps. This quote was written after his experience in the war. Now, that's a humbling perspective. While suffering the most profound misery that human beings can inflict on one another, Victor Frankl courageously chose the meaning he assigned to his experiences in the concentration camp. Consequently, he lived a much more resilient life post-war than many other survivors did, including becoming an author that inspired millions of others who have experienced tragedies and challenges to create their own meaning.

How did he do it? How did he get to this realization? Well, as a psychiatrist, he was inclined to reflect and observe his own thinking and as a result, was better able to generate a meaning that was effective for him and his situation.

Reflection and feedback are the most invaluable tools to create meaning, and I've experienced their power in every field that I've used them in.

Find time to reflect and learn from others' feedback.

During my time in the Army, our brigade flew each year to the National Training Center at Fort Irwin, California, where we performed large-scale maneuvers that sometimes involved thousands of soldiers and vehicles. After each training event, the unit conducted post-operation debriefings, which were called After Action Reviews, or AAR.

We asked ourselves, during the AAR, questions such as: What did we intend? What actually happened? What did we do well that we will sustain? What did we not do well that we will change? This form of reflection gave us, through hindsight, more insight into what had happened that day. And that's how we learned—through large-scale self-reflection—how to have more foresight.

These sorts of after-the-fact unpackings of events aren't limited to the military or other large organizations. They're necessary to maintain healthy relationships with our partners, our children, and our friends.

Early in our marriage, my wife and I would fight way more than was good for either of us. And early on, like with most couples, we could have been more "skillful" during our fights. We had resolved that we would never go to bed angry, an old chestnut of advice that I still think has been one of the most important pieces of our successful marriage, but that required conducting a sort of "meta-fight," where we would talk about what had gone wrong before (and during, sometimes) the fight.

For us, everything must be processed and resolved in the same day. It wasn't unlike the AAR in some ways, although the sparks weren't as explosive as in the Army. Here are some of the relationship-based questions that we would reflect on:

What happened?

What was the trigger?

What's your perspective?

What's mine?

What's the short-term solution?

What's the bigger issue?

How do we fight "better" in the future?

In this way, thinking about our fighting also required us to think about our thinking. And that type of metacognition is what helps us grow. In fact, it's a huge part of what makes us human. We're the only species that's even aware that we're thinking.

If you sit for one minute, doing nothing but watching yourself and your thoughts, it can feel like an eternity. This is a clue that quiet reflection doesn't come naturally to you—at least not currently. Good news: We get better at whatever we choose to do with our time. If self-awareness feels hard, it's because you're not used to it. But if you make time every day to reflect on yourself, your goals, and your progress, you'll find that your ability to observe yourself honestly will increase.

This isn't new and it isn't news. St. Ignatius was conducting a form of self-evaluation he called The Examen back in the 15th century.[11] He would spend roughly twenty minutes giving thanks, reviewing his day, facing his shortcomings, pondering corrective measures (and then selecting what he would do differently tomorrow), and then he would look ahead to the next day and plan. Then he would rely on feedback from his fellow worshippers, and also from his sense of his relationship with God.

Self-scrutiny is essential, but this doesn't mean that you should only limit your reflections to the present. Think about a one-week plan, and then a month, and then stretch it out into years. Then, see if your daily actions are aligned with the story you're trying to tell.

One of my favorite ways to track progress is journaling.

Time to Journal

When you commit to examining yourself in writing, you give yourself a chance to appreciate your own progress. A journal doesn't need to be about the mundane details of a day, but rather, small stories and moments you don't want to forget, and a record of your own achievements and frustrations. There is no progress without memory, and a journal will serve as your memory when your cranial software fails you. On that note, if you never make incremental progress, you never get to be proud of what you've done! A journal of your striving is *proof* that you've made progress, and you get to be proud of it!

Journaling can also remind you that things will always improve. Writing honestly about your life means writing about the bad times. At our lowest points, it's easy to forget that things were ever good, or to imagine that they could be good again. Looking through a journal during your bluest hour is a way of acknowledging that things weren't always this way, because *there are the words saying otherwise right in front of you, in your own hand.*

Time to Enlist Some Feedback

The other critical facet of examining yourself is asking for feedback, like Claire did when she flopped into the chair in my office. This can be tough, because you want to ask people who will be honest with you. If you're lacking in some areas, an honest person will let you know. When you ask for feedback, you forfeit the right to defensiveness, as long as the feedback is honest. Your job is to consider whatever is said to you. If you do this with enough people, how could it not change your perspective of yourself? You can only hear the same thing from so many people before you have to start taking them at their word.

Self-awareness is the key to telling the right story. Without it, it's kind of like reading a book with the pages out of order, hoping that it will all make sense in the end.

Self-reflection is the soul of wisdom. ~ Balthasar Gracian

Key Lesson: *Take a step back to reflect.*

Key Points:
- *Our lives are driven by our narratives.*
- *We can make our own meaning.*
- *Find time to reflect and learn from others' feedback.*

Action Steps for Learning

Action 1: Weekly "Down-Time"

Take an hour a week. In that hour, don't do any "productive work." Give yourself time and space. Go for a walk along your favorite path. Ride a bike around on a trail. Watch the sunset. If you noticed a nature theme, that's intentional. Nature helps. Use the time to "process." When you take your mind off of "doing mode," you give it chance to be free. During that time, you may find that all kinds of creative ideas come to you. (Incidentally, this also the reason why you get a lot of great ideas in the shower.)

Action 2: Asking for Feedback from Others

Ask ten people to give four words to describe you, one of which must be a word that describes an area where you could improve. I guarantee you that you will learn something that will help you.

Action 3: Journaling

In medical education, many students I know journal about something they've learned that day, or something that they're grateful for (which leads to resilience). There's a body of evidence that journaling leads to learning and creativity.[12] It's a practice that many leaders do as a part of their routine. It would be difficult to document the whole field of journaling here. Google "journaling practice." There will be examples that you will be able to adapt for your own practice.

Notes on Other Actions

What other actions could you take?

Worksheet: Limiting Narrative

- We all secretly have a narrative in our minds. Often, this narrative limits and hinders our fulfillment of our purpose.

- In the left dialogue box, write down the narratives in your mind that limit you. Be as negative and nasty as you can.

- In your narrative, address the following aspects: Work, Family, Health, Friends, Happiness.

- Now in the right dialogue box, rewrite the narrative from the left box to a new narrative which serves you and your purpose

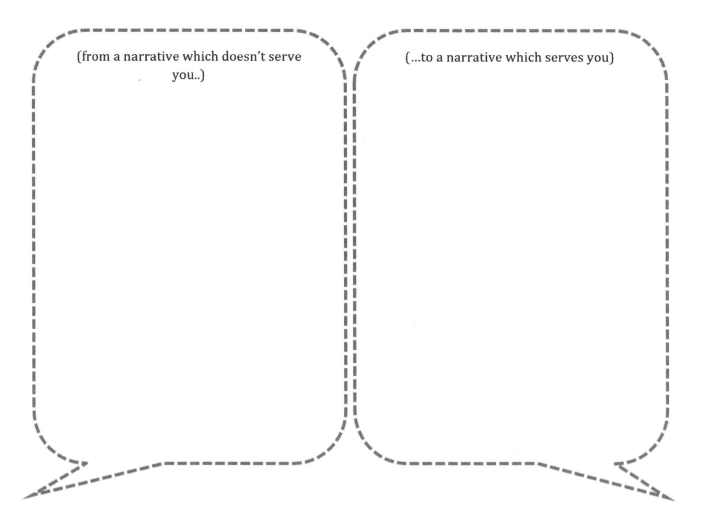

(from a narrative which doesn't serve you..)

(...to a narrative which serves you)

Word Problems: Self-Awareness = ?

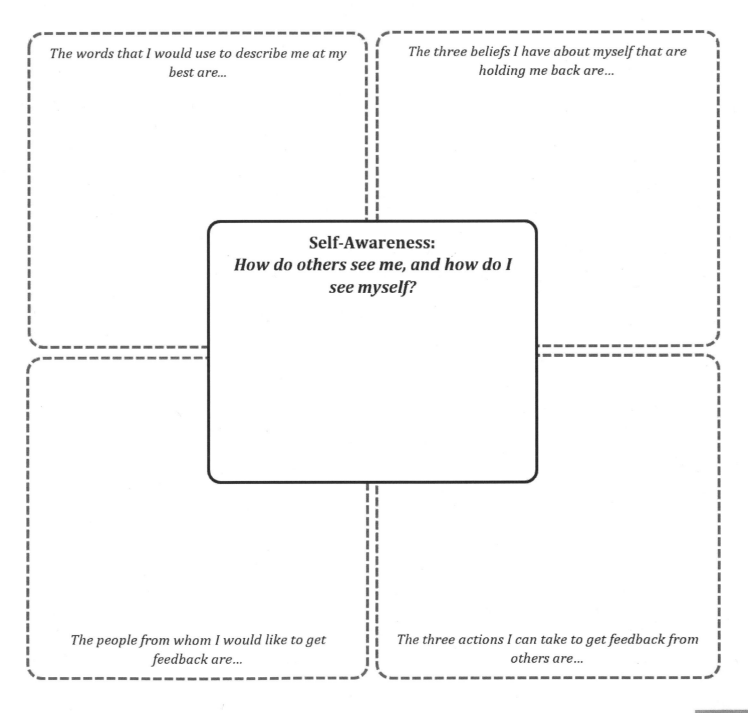

The words that I would use to describe me at my best are...

The three beliefs I have about myself that are holding me back are...

Self-Awareness:
How do others see me, and how do I see myself?

The people from whom I would like to get feedback are...

The three actions I can take to get feedback from others are...

Developing Your Unique Formula: the MEANING Domain

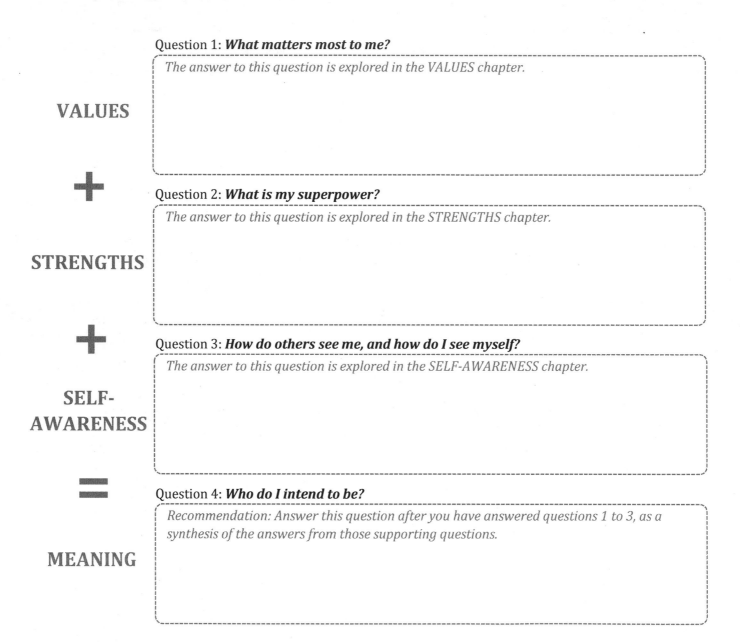

VALUES

Question 1: *What matters most to me?*

The answer to this question is explored in the VALUES chapter.

+

STRENGTHS

Question 2: *What is my superpower?*

The answer to this question is explored in the STRENGTHS chapter.

+

SELF-AWARENESS

Question 3: *How do others see me, and how do I see myself?*

The answer to this question is explored in the SELF-AWARENESS chapter.

=

MEANING

Question 4: *Who do I intend to be?*

Recommendation: Answer this question after you have answered questions 1 to 3, as a synthesis of the answers from those supporting questions.

DOMAIN:
COMMUNITY

- - - - - - - - - -

HOW WILL I SHOW UP FOR OTHERS?

*A deep sense of love and belonging is an irreducible need
of all people. We are biologically, cognitively, physically,
and spiritually wired to love, to be loved, and to belong.
When those needs are not met, we don't function as we were
meant to. We break. We fall apart. We numb. We ache.*

We hurt others. We get sick.

~ BRENE BROWN

How will I show up for others?

Empathy vs. Transaction:[13] See the Humanity in Others

Imagine for a moment that you have to sing your school's fight song in front of the whole student body. All alone, belting it out beneath the bright lights. How do you feel? Not too good, I would imagine. That's what it feels like when we see ourselves as separate from others, needing to defend ourselves. That's the 'little egoic me.' Now imagine that everyone is singing with you. You're not on the stage but in the crowd, adding your voice to the chorus. That's connection. That's community.

The paradox is that you have a harder time being your authentic self without community. When you're in the state of the 'little egoic' me, your focus can easily shift to defensiveness. You have to "puff" yourself up to feel adequate. You have to keep your guard up to ward off threats and protect yourself. In short, you have to distort yourself and pretend to be something that is not you.

But when you're part of a community, you can more easily let the walls come down. You can be yourself in a more natural way, because when you feel safe as part of a group, your thoughts can roam beyond yourself.

> *The human condition is one about belonging. We simply cannot thrive without belonging.* ~ John Powell

The connections humans make with each other are required for health, progress, and fulfillment; and you need to look no further than recent statistics for evidence of this.[14] [15]Despite all of the great material wealth we have access to in our culture, depression, substance abuse, suicide, and other malaises run rampant beneath the façade of our society. And research is beginning to show us how other people, like it or not, are the primary key to fighting these conditions. Communities matter, and you'll be far stronger in the right community for you than you would be on your own, provided that you understand how to be a positive influence in your group. We need connection with other people.

In the statement below, within the domain of community, we are not merely looking for personal success and achievement because in the absence of community, those things are meaningless.

Meaning ↓
Community ↰
Purpose ↰

To contribute your unique gift, while finding belonging in a caring community, to something meaningful that is greater than yourself.

We are looking to find belonging in a caring community. *Okay…so how do you get that?*

I've already shared my experience of college without this sense of belonging. It was awful to feel that alone. It wasn't until I was training with the other ROTC cadets that I felt anything like acceptance and belonging from peers. Where did it come from? Now, I'm no Clint Eastwood from "Heartbreak Ridge." It wasn't all guts and glory and machismo and bonding in foxholes, but it was one of the first moments when *I had responsibility for others*.

During one field training exercise, we had to march five miles in the snow with a thirty-pound ruck sack. Not fun, but it was harder on some than others. When I saw a fellow cadet struggling, I asked her if I could carry her ruck sack in addition to mine. She said yes, and I carried it for the rest of the march. I felt good to help. She felt good for being helped and finishing the exercise. In that instance, I felt like "myself" even more so than when I was by myself with the expressed purpose of "being myself." It was a fast and subtle, but incredibly important shift that occurred in me that day.

But what does this mean for you, and how do you make a shift like that?

When we were young, most of us were told to be nice to other people—to uphold the "golden rule" of doing unto others as we would have them do unto us. Those touchstones are indeed worthy, but we often have a difficult time putting them into practice. What is missing?

Empathy or Transaction?

Let's say you go to the grocery store and buy your weekly groceries. When you are at the checkout line, standing three feet away from the clerk as they scan your groceries, how do you see that person? Do you see him or her through a lens of *empathy*, as a full-on human being living his or her life? Or do you see him or her through a lens of *transaction*, where his or her full worth amounts to scanning your groceries?

Your perspective of this person will dictate how you "show up" for or relate to that person. Most importantly, the other person will *feel* your perspective regardless of the details of your interaction. If you see the *humanity* in them, they will *feel* it. If you do not, they will *feel* that as well.

The more you do of the former, the better your relationships will be.

In fact, how you "show up" for others dictates the quality of your community.

Domain: Community

How do you answer the question: *How will I show up for others?*

Take a look at the people in your life. All of them, not just the ones that "matter." What is the dominant lens through which you view people? Through the lens of *empathy*? Or through the lens of *transaction*? What intentions do you have about how you will "show up" for others which will lead you towards realizing your vision of community and belonging? . Before you can answer this question, consider the three "variables" below. These "variables" (network, relationship, communication) are fundamental pieces of this larger question of how you will show up for others.

Variables: Network, Relationship, Communication

Network: *What kind of people do I need to know?* (Variable 4)

You exist within a web of relationships, and all of those relationships influence you. Some relationships are supportive and some are toxic and hold you back. You have the ability to examine your network of relationships and shape it. What kind of network will help you be who and what you want to be? Where do you want to belong?

Relationships: *What's my way of building connection with others?* (Variable 5)

Think about your life. How do *you* build trust and connection? Are you a hard worker? Are you reliable? Do you meet every deadline? There will be something you do that not everyone does, and that will set you apart. In doing what sets you apart for the sake of others, you show up and contribute from your authentic self. Giving your authentic presence is a powerful way to create trust and build community.

Communication: *How do I communicate with influence?* (Variable 6)

Having a message isn't the same as having a message that is heard. And telling someone about your message isn't a guarantee that they will be influenced by it. Everything we do in groups communicates something. Body language, words, actions, the quality of your listening. As you get closer to living your values, you will have something to say—your message—that is of value to others. How will you communicate this message for understanding and impact?

The next three chapters are about "network," "relationships," and "communication"— the variables that will help you answer the question of how you will show up for others.

DOMAIN: COMMUNITY
Variable 4 =
NETWORK

- - - - - - - - - - - - - - - -

WHAT KIND OF PEOPLE DO I NEED TO KNOW?

*You are the average of the five people
you spend the most time with.*

~ JIM ROHN

Variable 4 = NETWORK

What kind of people do I need to know?

"So, where are you working now?" I asked a former classmate from business school who was standing at the bar next to me. She was a tall woman who always wore a wry smile, and always spoke her mind.

It was three years after we had graduated, and I had been looking forward to seeing her at this alumni gathering. Judy had been a star in our class—a very smart and ambitious woman—and had gone on to get a job on Wall Street.

"I'm at Louis Vuitton now," she replied, taking a sip from her cocktail. "I guess I didn't like the investment banking lifestyle." She scrunched her nose up in disgust for emphasis.

"So how did you make the switch? Doesn't Leah work at Louis Vuitton too?" I asked, knowing that she and Leah had been friends in school.

"Yes, in fact, I just sent Leah my resume, got an interview, and here I am." She took another sip and smiled.

I really prefer this stage of our career, I thought to myself as I tasted my drink. When we were in business school, we were "applying" for a job and had to rely on ourselves (for the most part) to prove our qualifications and interests. After business school, we didn't have to rely just ourselves. Those of us who had built a network of relationships came to realize quickly that it was much easier to find and land jobs when someone in the network offered a warm introduction.

"Do you remember how hard it was to apply for a job while we were in b-school? We had to jump through so many hoops to prove ourselves. It was such a long and tedious process, and a lot of us didn't even get the jobs we wanted. Now look at us. We can just change jobs with 10% of the effort." I shook my head at the difference.

"Yeah, we worked SO hard! I went to social events to make friends because I just wanted to have a social life. Of course it occurred to me that, maybe down the road, some of these friends may help out somehow, but I had no idea how fast they can come through. Had I known what I know now, I would have spent so much more time building relationships and so much less time stressing out in the library figuring out how to value derivatives." Judy laughed out loud at the idea.

"We'll you'll never know when you'll need to value a derivative." I laughed along with her, feeling especially grateful for the power of the network we had developed in school and since.

When you graduate from college, how much knowledge do you retain? Think about when you were studying intensely to pass a test. After the thrill of getting your good grade faded, the information you used to win scholastic glory probably faded as well. Two months after you took a test, how many of those facts were still in your head? Unless you were constantly using them, probably not many of them; and if you're like most students, that applies to nearly every assignment or test you took in nearly every class.

If your brain treats what you learn in classes this way, then there's not much difference between taking two classes or two dozen, right? If the information delivery system of college doesn't allow you to *keep* the information, what's the value of college?

So maybe we shouldn't focus on what we learn (and forget) while we're students. If the number of friends you made in college equaled the classes you took, is that more valuable? Absolutely! Even people that aren't highly memorable are still more memorable than most facts you learn to take tests. Maybe that's the real value of college. You may never be around that many variety of people again. There may *never* be another chance for you to form so many relationships, all in one place.

It can matter more than you might think, particularly when you're embarking on a career.

At the time of this writing, I'm forty-five years old. It's been almost twenty years since I had to "apply for a job" and do it on my own merits—earning it through grades, the right resume, a sparkling cover letter, etc. All the jobs and opportunities I've had since have been the direct result of opportunities that arose through the people in my network. Yes, I worked diligently, and that's still necessary, but few things were more valuable than learning how to accept help from others. And this became part of the work I was willing to do: Even though I was focused on doing a good job, I also took care to purposefully cultivate a mutually useful network of people. I can help them, they can help me, and it makes everything easier. It's true, but why is it true?

You become more like the people with whom you associate.

When I was in the Army, I did a lot of running as part of the physical training regimen. I improved with each run because that's just how it works, but it was always a struggle. Struggle or not, I had to be able to pass the physical exams. That meant running two miles in under sixteen minutes. Every year, I did what I had to so that I could beat that time. However, it was the pressure of the requirements that drove me. Well, that and the embarrassment I would have suffered if I had failed that test as an officer. It didn't hurt that nearly everyone in my unit was faster than I was either. They exerted a different sort of positive pressure on me, one that I couldn't have created or replicated on my own. *I ran faster in order to belong.*

A Pew research study showed that if one of your close friends or family members gets divorced, you're 75% more likely to get divorced. The number falls to 33% if you're two degrees of separation removed from the divorce, but that number should still feel inordinately high to someone who hopes for a happily-ever-after marriage. [16]

If someone close to you has a baby, then you're more likely to give birth or father a child.

If you start eating donuts, the chances of your friends eating donuts goes up, placing you at the middle of a sugary whirlwind that benefits none of you.

Given all of these facts, it probably won't surprise you to learn that if those in your inner circle have cardiovascular disease, you're at higher risk for it.[17] Why? Because, to the extent that cardiovascular disease is a function of certain behaviors, you're more likely to engage in the behaviors of the people you are closest to.

What about money? This is a good piece of news for those of you who surround yourselves with the financially secure. You're more likely to earn in the wage bracket of the people you associate with the most, and the most closely.

Personally, I can't think of many things that are more unappealing than chewing tobacco. Well, guess who started chewing tobacco when he was in the Army? This guy. When you're out in the field on maneuvers or drills, it gets boring. Chewing tobacco, as ridiculous as it sounds, is a way to pass the time. And when everyone else is doing it, well…soon you're spitting into a cup even though there was literally a 0% chance that you would have picked up the habit on your own.

Because there are positive and negative contagions, it's helpful to think of the people around you as carriers of certain habits, conditions, and aspirations. Assume that you will be exposed to them. This can be risky or rewarding, depending on the circles you participate in.

You are the average of the five people you spend the most time with.
~ Jim Rohn

I hate to be the one to break it to you—although you may already grasp it intuitively—but your friends don't really want you to improve. Maybe a little, but not too much. Well, why not? What kind of friend would that be? Sadly, the normal kind. This is just what it means to be human. The more you improve, the worse they might think or feel that your progress reflects on them, especially if they're not keeping pace. More bad news: You're probably no better, and neither am I.

Imagine that you and I are friends and co-workers. One day I show up at work and say, "Hey, got a minute? You know how neither of us hates this job, but neither of us loves it either even though we work so hard? Well, I'm quitting to start my own business. I'm also going to write a book."

Okay, how would it make you feel? I know how it might make me feel if you said it. I would probably feel bad for myself, and then feel the pressure beneath the question, "Why am *I* not doing that?"

Maybe, instead of encouraging each other in the new endeavor, we would try to keep each other down on behalf of the status quo. So, what do we do about this?

I was fortunate enough to grow up with people who challenged me. Anything I consider a success in my life is as much a result of the people who have influenced me as my own efforts. I didn't have to go out of my way to find them.

Not everyone has that luxury, of course. If you didn't grow up in a similar situation (as far as the people around you), but you want to surround yourself with people who will influence you in desirable ways, you have to go find them. You can "hang out" with intention, if you decide to. And to be as successful as possible, you must.

There are at least three ways that you can insert people of influence into your life. First, the direct approach—get out there and meet like-minded people, or people whose goals are similar to yours.

Second, you should read about people you would like to emulate in both personality and results. Biographies about people like Abraham Lincoln and Theodore Roosevelt have fired me up to the point where my middle son's name is Lincoln and my youngest son's name is Theodore. Reading about someone—in depth, not on Wikipedia—creates a type of relationship with them. Immerse yourself in a person and their ideas, and you'll internalize some of the virtues that characterized them. How could it be otherwise, unless you deliberately commit to not doing so? People do not have to be physically present to inspire you, which brings us to point three.

Visualize them. When I need guidance, I can always go to my inner circle and ask them to weigh in, but I also find it helpful to visualize a council of people I admire and ask myself how I think they would respond to me. I imagine what advice they might have. Stories they might tell. Conclusions they might draw. Think about who would be on your imaginary council and do the same.

Does any of this sound a little uncomfortable? I know it probably does, but it's important because a network of varied influencers will contribute to your growth and success.

Different people contribute in different ways.

Now let's go beyond five people. You can learn from anyone. So can I. When I was working as a career advisor, I often told job seekers that if they wanted to find a new job, they needed to tell thirty people about their intentions. In addition to work and smarts, creating opportunities also takes some luck. Telling thirty people what they were looking for was an easy, surefire way to increase their luck and, therefore, their potential opportunities.

If you're thinking that thirty people is a lot, or that you don't know that many people, then I have some good news for you: You know more people than you think. You're probably only thinking about the people closest to you. Most of us don't have thirty people in our inner circle, so you have to go wider.

Think of your network as three rings. [18]

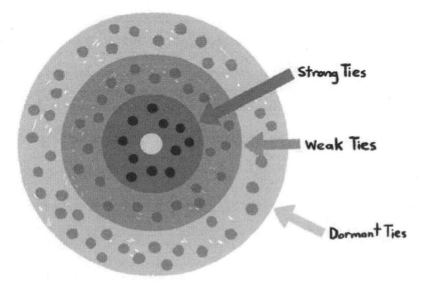

Strong Ties

Weak Ties

Dormant Ties

The **strong ties** are your strongest relationships. Family, close friends, and mentor figures. They're the obvious choice, but they're also the people most likely to help maintain the status quo in your life.

Weak ties are the relationships that are closer to the acquaintance level. They are people you could become closer to, but your current relationships with them are pleasant, though somewhat superficial. These offer more potential, because they are relationships in the exploratory phase. You don't know what you might find if you delve into them.

Dormant ties could be people you've lost track of completely. They've probably changed since the last time you spoke, and you probably have too. Reconnecting with them will transform them into weak ties, which then have the potential to become strong ties. And because each person will also know other people, growing your circle is simple, even if it doesn't feel easy. Once you know more people, there are more questions you can find answers to, because you'll know people with an increasing range of expertise.

If you want to start a new exercise regimen, are you more likely to find a fitness junkie in a circle of five people, or thirty?

If you want to start a new company, are you more likely to find a firebrand entrepreneur in a smaller network, or a larger one?

It's a no-brainer. But network can be a sterile, meaningless word. Let's call it a team instead.

The goal of your team, as far as you're concerned for this exercise, is to help you win—to help you reach your goal. This doesn't mean they're pawns in your game, whose only purpose is to elevate you, but you get the gist. On a baseball team, everyone plays a different role. The pitcher pitches. The center fielder doesn't wander in from the outfield to take charge of first base. The catcher doesn't swap with the shortstop. They all have a role.

To achieve your goal, what roles would you need your team members to play for you? If you were a talent scout looking for prospective team members, you might come up with something this this:[19]

Expert practitioners

Professional peers with high standards

People to provide feedback

People who will hold you accountable

People with whom you can share ideas

Roles models and mentors

Emotional supporters, providers of safety

Senior sponsors

Anyone with industry or community connections

There can obviously be some overlap between roles, and this list could be much longer, but hopefully you see the benefit to this approach. Now, *you* try it. Take five minutes and write down twenty names. Then, see if you can assign roles to them based on your understanding of their strengths.

The flipside is that there will always be people who influence us negatively, or who have the potential to do so. Being in the world means that we can't always decide exactly who passes in and out of our orbit. Even in the strongest, most supportive families, it's not perfectly harmonious from dawn to dusk. People get on each other's nerves. So what should we do when this happens? We have to have this answer, because this is just reality.

In a true community we will not choose our companions, for our choices are so often limited by self-serving motives. Instead, our companions will be given to us by grace. Often, they will be persons who will upset our settled view of self and world. In fact, we might define true community as the place where the person you least want to live with always lives. ~ Parker Palmer

You're not going to click with everyone, but that does not mean you can't learn from the proverbial thorns in your side. But what can you learn? I'd recommend trying to treat every relationship, whether it lasts for a minute or decades, as a gift. Ask yourself, "Why would someone give me this gift?" This will force you to see what you can learn from it. Challenges trigger collapse or growth. You can choose your own adjective, but abrasive, uncooperative, arrogant, vindictive, myopic people can show you something about yourself too. Jung argued that when you see a trait in someone that you just can't stand, it's something that may exist in you that you would rather keep secret. If they don't bring anything else to your life, they may simply be opportunities for deeper self-reflection and growth.

You can only work on and change yourself, but you must invest in your network.

"Invest" in your network.

Just to give you an idea about how seriously I take this, I *schedule* time on Fridays to think about my friends. It's that important to me.

As you know by now, I'm not a naturally outgoing person. If I didn't set aside time to ponder friendships, I'd forget and wind up watching a bug or reading.

(I'm that kid in the front doing my own thing - looking at a bug)

Every Friday, I look at the "list" of people in my network. Who am I hanging out with more these days? Who am I neglecting? Who do I need to reach out to? What have I been invited to? What should I invite someone to? If our family friends are having a get-together, I make a point of reminding myself that I need to accept all social invitations. It's not because I'm trying to get something out of people. It's how I acknowledge the importance of connection with others. I dedicate time to it, intentionally, which is the clearest signal I can give myself that I'm serious about it.

There's a literal wealth to be found in the size and quality of your network, or your team. You can have $10 million in the bank and still be miserable, yet it's hard to find someone who has many close friends and unconditional support who isn't happy. And, because we are looking at our network (team) as a type of wealth, we can approach it as we would any investment.

Whatever you appreciate in your life, 'appreciates' in value. ~ John Demartini

Financial wealth must be managed. You have to review your income and spending. You have to review your balances. You have to review your portfolio of investments. You have to be intentional about where you put your savings. And you need to do all of these things all the time, reevaluating and adjusting as things change. It takes energy, but it's worth it if the wealth grows and your freedom expands accordingly.

Toward the end of our conversation, Judy and I explored a brilliant idea.

"If networking was one of the keys to opportunity, why don't we have a class in business school on networking just so that we do it right?" I wondered out loud.

"Oh my God, that would be the best class ever! I'd take that class in a heartbeat! It would be even more important than finance. Wait...yeah it would!" Judy exclaimed.

"We'll, I'd take that same class every semester, because I'm introverted and would need a lot more practice to outdo you!" I laughed.

Wouldn't that be amazing?

But don't just invest in your team....

Invest in yourself (too).

Obviously, you can't only invest in other people. Everything mentioned in the previous section also goes for your health, your education (in the classroom and outside of it), and your family. You know what you have to do to nurture these pursuits. Dollars, calories, pounds on the barbell, miles run, pages read and written, and minutes spent in quiet contemplation all add up. So does the effort of investing in meaningful, intentional connections. You must think, and plan, and experiment, and execute, gauge your results, tweak your process, and then you do it again, over and over until you're satisfied. And by the time you're satisfied, you'll probably have new goals that will require the same process.

This is a good thing, because stagnation will cease to be a reality for you. You can be whoever you want to be, and much of that is a result of who you surround yourself with. Go find them. You'll not regret it.

> **Key Lesson:** *Define and expand your social circle.*
>
> **Key Points:**
> - *You become more like the people you associate with.*
> - *Different people contribute in different ways.*
> - *"Invest" in your network.*

Action Steps for Learning

Action 1: Join / Start a Club

Go find your tribe. They are out there. Do you want to start your own business? Do you enjoy reading about history? Do you like cooking (or eating)? There are people who share your interests. Find a way to connect with them through clubs or meetups, or create your own group.

Action 2: Coffee / Lunch with New People

For the next two months, have lunch or coffee once per week with one person you don't currently know well. If you are looking to make larger changes in your life, have lunch or coffee with two (or more) per week.

Action 3: Engage Mentors

In your academic or professional settings, there are plenty of people who can help you. They have already been through a lot of what you are about to go through. If you have an idea about something, they can help you shape that idea. What mentors often want is someone who wants to listen to them. Be a good listener, and be willing to learn. Of course, be discerning in who you choose as mentors.

Notes on Other Actions

What other actions could you take?

Worksheet: The Five People

Part A. Five People (Current)

Who are the five people you currently have the most contact with? Indicate the names of those five people in the box below. For each person, reflect on whether they influence you to grow, remain in the status quo, or regress. Place a dot on the continuum line to indicate their influence.

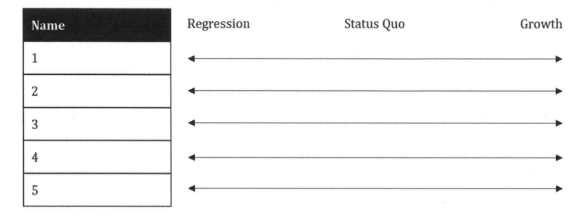

Part B. Five Characteristics

What are the five characteristics that you are looking to enhance within yourself? Please indicate those characteristics below. Then, ask yourself, Who are people who embody those characteristics? (They can be people that you know, or people that you know of but do not know personally.) Indicate those names next to the corresponding characteristics.

Characteristics	Names
1.	
2.	
3.	
4.	
5.	

Worksheet: Your Supportive Network

Category (e.g. role models)	Maintain People you already know that you should maintain contact with	Develop People you know of but should get to know better	Explore People (or categories of people) who you should reach out to

Word Problems: Network = ?

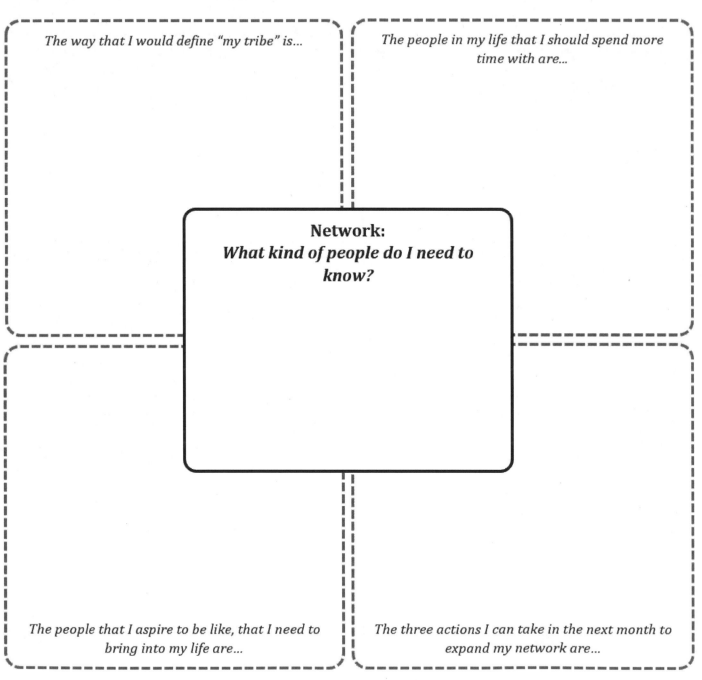

The way that I would define "my tribe" is...

The people in my life that I should spend more time with are...

Network:
What kind of people do I need to know?

The people that I aspire to be like, that I need to bring into my life are...

The three actions I can take in the next month to expand my network are...

DOMAIN: COMMUNITY

Variable 5 =
RELATIONSHIPS

- - - - - - - - - -

WHAT'S MY WAY TO BUILD CONNECTION WITH OTHERS?

With rare exceptions, all of your most important achievements on this planet will come from working with others—or, in a word, partnership.

~ PAUL FARMER

Variable 5 = RELATIONSHIPS

What's my way to build connection with others?

"I'm just running out the clock til graduation," Mark grimaced. He was a smart but reserved business school student who I bumped into from time to time. When he asked to meet me for coffee, I was happy to make time in my schedule.

"It doesn't sound like school is going all that great," I reflected, taking a closer look at his deflated demeanor.

He shrugged. "I'm doing well in class. The professors are great. Don't get me wrong. It's just that I don't enjoy my classmates very much. Business school students are always partying and drinking. It's hard for me to get into that kind of stuff. I just don't feel like myself in those situations." He looked down at his coffee.

Ah yes. Let's see what he does with this.

"Aren't you being kind of selfish, Mark?" I asked.

Taken aback, he looked up at me with wide eyes. "What do you mean?"

"What do your classmates get for getting to know Mark? Do they get a shy, awkward classmate? You're focused on 'poor you.' What do they get?" I challenged him.

"I'm still not tracking you," he said, obviously struggling to see where I was going.

"You're saying that you're not quite 'yourself' in those party situations. In what situations would you rather know your classmates? Think about situations where you are more 'yourself' and look for ways to be of value to others in *that* way." I paused a moment to let the idea sink in before pressing with another question. "So, when are you most 'yourself?'"

Smiling as the understanding flooded him, he took a moment before answering. "I'm good at taking notes and leading study groups. I was a TA for a few classes and can explain difficult concepts so that my classmates understand them."

"Well, let's talk about some ways you can do more of that in your interactions with your classmates—where they can get to know you at your best."

After a few minutes of brainstorming, he promised to do more to help his classmates, and then we turned our chat to lighter topics while we finished our coffee.

(three months later)

"Mark, how's school?" I asked as our paths crossed in the hallway.

"It's going great! I'm still doing well grade-wise, but I have so many people asking for my help. I've also been invited to a bunch of parties, and I think people actually like me. I still don't think I'll ever be completely comfortable at b-school parties, but I'll live with that." The big smile on his face told me that he'd found his way.

"I'm glad to hear that. Whenever you see yourself focusing on 'poor me,' think about how you can be of value to others. By the way, I was always a wallflower at parties." I laughed and patted his back before heading to my office.

"Good to know!" He smiled as we parted ways.

Often, when our relationships aren't the way we want them, it's something that we are failing to be or to do. We are often not bringing the best of ourselves to the people around us. We don't extend our trust and receive trust. We focus on ourselves and what we're *not* getting instead of focusing on how we can provide value to others.

When we focus on giving of our authentic selves to others, our relationships revive and thrive. We find the connection and community we have been craving.

But how do we make that shift?

It's all about trust.

This may seem a cliché, but I learned a lot about trust in the Army. When I was twenty-two, I was a platoon leader for a unit of four tanks and sixteen soldiers—soldiers that were about as different as people can be. One was a former gang leader from the south side of Chicago who joined the Army to escape the heat of the police. Another one was a small town garage mechanic from Texas. It goes on and on. There were no other Ivy League nerds besides myself.

Yet, we were a close-knit group. When someone in the unit got a DUI, I would bail them out of jail. When there was a domestic dispute, we would go in and help settle the tempers. How did this happen? I can't imagine another circumstance where this odd assortment of sixteen people would have the cohesion to do anything together. We were different people from different walks of life with different viewpoints. We couldn't even agree whether O.J. Simpson was guilty.

The one thing that we did have in common was that we were all soldiers of the third platoon in Charlie Company. We all went out to the field together. We ate the same food. We all endured the same miseries of military life. We all wore the same uniform. We shared many **things in common**; and THAT was a key reason why, despite our vast differences, we still had trust in one another.

If you're looking to build trust, first **establish the commonalities**. These days, things seem to be so focused on differences, especially on university campuses. This focus on diversity has, in many ways, exacerbated the perceived differences among people within a school's community. While I do believe that differences should be appreciated, it may be counterproductive to begin with the differences, instead of the commonalities. Before we establish our commonality, differences are threatening. In order for us to appreciate each other's differences, we must first appreciate our commonality. As an example, if all I know is that you are a conservative (or liberal) and I am of the opposite political view, then it becomes very difficult for me to empathize with you. However, if I know your story, your background, and the places where we share common ground in life, I am more open to appreciate our differences.

If nothing else, we are all people—all wired much more similarly than differently. We all want generally similar things—love, belonging, purpose, vision. We all need similar things.

Having been an immigrant, I know the feeling of being different. As a result, I've doubled down on my effort to find commonality with those in my community (who after all, aren't Chinese immigrants). I find that it is practically guaranteed that I can find commonality with anyone that I talk to, from a preference in books, places that we've visited, groups that we belong to, to just being in the same room talking and sharing a common experience.

A second element of trust that I learned from my experience in the military is **vulnerability**. As a military unit, we were dependent on each other for safety. The spoken and unspoken code was: "When you go to sleep, I'm on watch. When you look this way and cover my back, I look that way and cover your back. I am placing my life in your hands, and I know you are placing yours in mine."

That is vulnerability.

Of course, we don't need to literally place our lives in the hands of others to build trust. However, we do need to place something that we care about in the hands of others. This could be a fear, an emotion, a desire.

When Mark and I talked about his student experience, he allowed me to challenge him. Why? Because we had developed trust. The common basis for our trust was that we were both looking out for his best interest. The common ground allowed him to place a certain level of vulnerability in my care; and as a result, although what I had to say was hard to hear, our trust enabled that authentic communication that led to him creating a better experience for himself.

When we summon the **courage to be vulnerable**, we place our trust in another. This is not easy to do. We can't know for sure that our vulnerability will be accepted by the other. However, it is a powerful act. More often than not, people reciprocate. You've taken the chance to build trust. Over time, you will be rewarded with relationships built on trust.

Speaking of reciprocity…

Focus more on giving than getting.

Compared to the distant past, we have more of everything today. We have more of everything today than we did yesterday, for that matter. Actually, you know what? I bet that while I was writing this paragraph, at least one new flavor of Doritos sprang into being.

Well, good for us. Look at all of the stuff out there. But it's not making us happier. Focusing on getting stuff means focusing on you, but not in a healthy way. It's the process of forging your identity through what you can acquire, not by contemplating who you are and might one day be.

There's no better way to get out of your own head than to help someone else. It may be impossible to obsess over getting while you are giving.

Adam Grant wrote an amazing book called *Give and Take*, in which he defines three categories of people: Givers, Matchers, and Takers.[20]

First, let's define them.

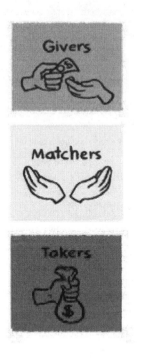

The Givers give. They put more effort into giving than into taking. Simple.

The Takers take. In an organization full of takers, it's not uncommon for everyone to appear successful, but the success of a taker tends to occur at the expense of others.

The Matchers are somewhere in between. They give and take, but they also tend to reflect the category of people by which they are surrounded.

Grant studied various organizations and determined the percentages of these three groups within each one. He then used the data to determine which of these three categories seemed to account for the most productive, successful organizations.

Interestingly, the highest and lowest performing people in each organization were Givers. How might we account for that? Well, think about someone you know who you would consider a Giver. Maybe your person is generous, but is also a doormat who can be taken advantage of. Givers are notorious people-pleasers and are often better at giving to others than giving to themselves. These Givers account for the lowest performing people.

The highest performing Givers give from a position of strength. To start with, they know what their strengths are. They're not cynical mercenaries, but they give with an agenda. They are aware that giving leads to more giving, and that they will ultimately benefit from the generosity they show to others. These Givers are also adept at keeping their distance from Takers.

You don't have to believe in literal Karma to know that what goes around comes around. The history of psychology is a massive argument for the fact that none of us truly get away with anything. We pay a psychic cost for every decision we make, and the cost can be a reward or a punishment, depending on our motives. Conversely, when we act in the spirit of genuine generosity, situations and people will orient themselves to us. Our luck seems to improve because we created a small change in a world that is now positioned to favor our efforts.

When you give strategically—and again, I don't mean from a standpoint of selfishness or manipulation—you'll maximize your efforts and the positive effects you have on others.

In fact, you might even find that you can begin to appreciate and even love everyone who crosses your path.

Love everyone. (You can only work on yourself.)

A few years ago, I was listening to an audiobook by Ram Dass, a spiritual teacher I've greatly admired. During his training, one of his gurus had given him a simple—not easy!—precept upon which to meditate. "Love everyone and tell the truth." In the beginning, Ram Dass found that he could only do one of the two. He often had misgivings about people in his spiritual community, and during those times, he could either put on a "happy face" or be brutally candid in his annoyance. It was a ton of work to integrate the two experiences. But given what we've already talked about in this chapter, it should be clear that building trust—via telling the truth, giving, and admitting vulnerability—may be the only thing that makes loving everyone possible.

Okay, so this is a tall order. It might even be impossible. Love everyone. Everyone? For this chapter, assume that, even if you *can't* love everyone, *it's possible to act as if you do.* If you act as if you love anyone, perhaps it can become a reality for you. If not, there's still no downside. Acting as if you love people massively simplifies problems.

It's easy to love people who support us. Our supporters help us. They probably sound like we do, and they may share the same concerns and attitudes. It's easy to love people who affirm the things you think you know. But there are also people who challenge us, make us grind our teeth, remind us that foolishness exists, test our patience, and…well, let's just charitably say that there are people we "love" less.

Life doesn't happen to you. It happens for you. ~ Jim Carrey

It's useful to look at exactly why and how these challenging people challenge us. In fact, growth comes from examining the challenges that other people present, and figuring out just what about them is so maddening. And if you can make yourself step towards them, continually, by degrees, trying to understand, you will expand your limits without bashing up against them.

If you spend much time thinking about how life needs to be different in order for you to be happy, may I gently suggest that perhaps life is already in balance, and you might get more out of learning to see differently? Perhaps the support and challenges in your life are already balanced and optimized for your growth?

Let's work with a solid career example here, since this is a conversation I have repeatedly with people discussing careers.

Jedi-Level Career Advice (Gratitude = Graduation)[21]

When you enter a new situation, or just being in your current situation, you will notice that you will have challenges and support. There will be some people with whom you will clash (challenge), and some people with whom you will get along well (support).

Initially, you will infatuate with your supporters and despise your challengers. You will wish to yourself, "How can I have more of my supporters' warm embrace and less of my challengers' stinging barbs?" But this is not seeing things clearly for what they are.

Your challengers will push your buttons. They will challenge you. You will want to change them, or your will want to run away from them. But neither approach here will work. People are hard to change. If you run away, you will just re-encounter the same challenging lesson in a different person.

Eventually, the futility of trying to change others or to run away will prompt you to work on yourself. How can I protect my buttons? What am I supposed to be learning about myself? How is this challenging situation actually helping me?

Bingo. That's the insight.

You realize that all those challenges have actually been prompting you to up your game. All those criticisms about your presentation actually prompted you to make a better presentation. All those doubts about your ability actually prompted you to get better. ("I'll show him.") All those opinions you disagree with actually made you more aware of what you believed in. The challenger was helping you!

When you understand this, it's hard not to be grateful for both the challenges and the support. You see things for what they actually are—balanced and perfect for your optimal growth.

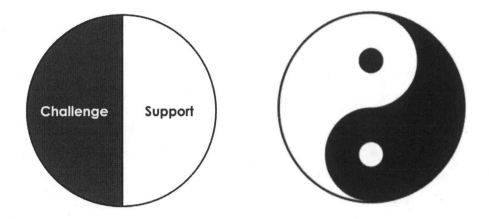

When the current situation is no longer challenging us to grow, what happens? You will "graduate" to a higher level of challenge. Life will give you a harder lesson to challenge your growth. Often, this will take the form of an actual promotion where you will face a new set of people (challengers and supporters) at a higher level.

In the beginning, you will fall back into the trap of infatuating with your supporters and despising your challengers. This is entirely normal, but after so many of these promotions, you may begin to have this inkling that perhaps your job is not just to "do your job," but to see the situation for what it is: balanced and perfect for your optimal growth.

So, you work on yourself. You protect your buttons. You clarify your resolve. You grow. You see how the situation was "perfect" for your growth all along. You feel gratitude. You begin to "graduate" again…

Remember Mark and his challenge in connecting with his classmates? He had to transform the way he saw his classmates from a "me vs. them" lens to a "me helping them" lens. As a result, the situation became balanced. This happened not because others changed the way they behaved, but because Mark was able to change himself.

The rewards are great.

> **Key Lesson:** *Build Trusting Relationships.*
>
> **Key Points:**
> - *It's all about trust.*
> - *Focus more on giving than getting.*
> - *Love everyone. (You can only work on yourself.)*

Action Steps for Learning

Action 1: Be a Better Listener

One of the most important things you can give someone is your attention. One of the ways to do that is through your listening. We all know that we can get better at that. So pick a few people with whom you would like to improve your relationship, and when you're with them, focus on your listening. Listen with your ears, but also listen with your eyes and your whole body. Try to understand their point of view instead of formulating what you want to say. Your relationship with that person is bound to improve.

Action 2: When meeting with others, focus on "how I can be of service" to that person.

A second strategy to improve your relationships is to focus on how you might be of service to that other person. By default, we are thinking about what we want. Instead, think about how this interaction can benefit the other person. Place that intention in your mind prior and during the engagement.

Action 3: Meditate

If you develop a disciplined habit of daily meditation, you will find that you will have greater access to the relaxation response during interactions, which will allow you to maintain presence and composure during interactions, especially heated ones.

Notes on Other Actions

What other actions could you take?

Word Problems: Relationships = ?

The ways that I naturally connect with people is through...

The situations which most easily "trigger" me are...

Relationships:
What's my way to build connection with others?

The words that describe the way I want to treat other people is...

The ways that I can provide more value to my relations are...

DOMAIN: COMMUNITY
Variable 6 =
COMMUNICATION

- - - - - - - - - - - - - -

HOW DO I COMMUNICATE WITH INFLUENCE?

*Man's inability to communicate is a result
of his failure to listen effectively.*

~ CARL ROGERS

How do I communicate with influence?

"I'm nervous about my presentation tomorrow," Beth admitted as she fidgeted, trying to get comfortable in the chair sitting on the other side of my desk.

I smiled at the petite, fashionably-dressed woman sitting across from me as I waited for her to continue. She was an energetic emergency medicine doctor who was embarking on an academic career, focused on researching problems relating to healthcare access. The next day, she and a few colleagues were scheduled to present her research work to a group of research experts in healthcare.

"What if they ask a question I can't answer?" Beth looked up from her clenched fists on her lap.

I have no doubt her research is solid, but I totally understand the feeling of intimidation when it comes to presenting in front of an expert audience, I thought to myself as I formulated my response.

"How many academic conferences have you attended?" I asked.

"Six or seven," she answered quickly.

"How many talks have you listened to in those six or seven conferences?" I wondered.

"Almost too many to count. Definitely more than fifty," she responded.

"Well, in those fifty-plus talks, how much of the content do you remember?" I probed for more information to make my point.

"Very little. Almost none, to tell you the truth," she said, eyebrows now raised with wonder at my line of inquiry.

"Do you remember a few of the speakers?" I asked.

She glanced out the window as she searched for the right words. "Yes, there were a few who were memorable. It felt like they were less about telling us about what they did, and more engaging in a dialogue with us."

"Are you passionate about why you are doing this research?" I asked rhetorically, smiling as I recalled the many hours I had spent listening to her share about her findings.

Sitting up a little straighter in her chair, she answered confidently: "Yes, I am dedicated to this work and to helping make healthcare more accessible to those in need."

"How would you have to give your presentation so that I *'feel'* and share that passion with you? Don't think too much about the words, but think on how you must *'feel'* during the presentation."

"I will definitely have to work on that part of my talk," she said, smiling at the idea. "It's true that it's easy for us researchers to get stuck in our heads while we are sharing data, isn't it?"

I nodded my agreement.

"Thank you for the reminder to stay connected to the passion that is driving this research. I really appreciate your time." She grabbed her purse and stood up to leave.

"Of course. Any time. I know you're going to nail the presentation tomorrow."

The next day, I grinned from ear-to-ear as I watched her deliver a talk that was full of passion and engagement. The smiles and hearty clapping by the panel of experts showed how impressed they were.

It isn't about words. It's never about the words, I thought to myself as I walked back to my office.

When we think about communication, we often think about words. More specifically, we focus on the words that we will use to tell somebody something.

However, there's more to communication than using words to transfer of information. To communicate is to build understanding, with both parties understanding an issue, a problem, or even making the world a little better for having spoken.

If not only words, then what?

Communication starts with your state.

Imagine that you're at a party. Oh! That person you've always wanted to meet is there! You rehearse something witty in your head, wipe your sweaty palms, walk over, and start a conversation.

How long do you think it takes for that person to form an impression of you? Or a distinct opinion about whether they like you or not? A lot can be conveyed in a few seconds, and this person probably started sizing you up before you started talking. A few sentences into the conversation, this person already has—or thinks they have—an idea of what you're like, even though you haven't said much yet. But you're always communicating, and what is communicated constantly is what we will call your "state." Call it your vibe, confidence (or lack of), your aura, or the way you carry yourself. It all says something about you.

We'll come back to the party in a bit. Let's say that you're about to go in for a job interview. You've been lusting after this position and now it's finally your time to show and tell them that they'd be insane not to hire you. The interviewer emerges from the boardroom, shakes your hand, and says hello. You blurt out something that is obviously scripted and is possibly a non-sequitur to the greeting you just received. What is the interviewer now thinking about you?

Or say that you're the one doing the interviewing. You're choosing which of two auto mechanics will fix your car. Mechanic one fidgets like he's covered in ants, swallows constantly, can't meet your eyes, and looks like he'd rather be anywhere than engaging in human contact.

The other mechanic listens closely, restates what you've said, asks questions that shows he has understood your problem, and confidently tells you that he knows what to do.

Who are you going to hire?

With the interview scenario, the interviewer has probably formed a strong impression of you within the first minute. Consider that you're not the only candidate. When all else is equal, interviewers have to look for something to break the tie between prospective employees. The employee who wins is usually the one who spent at least as much time considering *how* they present themselves, as they did preparing the "right" answers to potential questions.

Wit never hurts. Good looks are always welcome. But the first, substantive impressions of you will always come from what you communicate about your inner state.

By the way, you don't have to be standing in front of someone to give them an unfavorable impression of your inner state, either. Imagine that you wake up after a long, restless night to an email from a coworker, saying that you didn't complete a critical task on time. Worse, your boss is CC'd on the email. Instantly, you're angry. For one, the deadline wasn't clear, so this really isn't your mistake. And this isn't how you wanted to start your day! How dare this person curse you with their fussing seconds after you get out of bed!

Okay, then. How should you respond? How many times have you sent an angry email? How many times did the result make you say, "Wow! It worked out perfectly. From now on, I only send angry emails!"

Right. Never.

Email seems neutral because people can deal with each other at a distance, but nuance and presentation still matter. In the wrong state, email can be even more of a danger to effective communication because it can feel consequence-free in a way that face-to-face interactions rarely do. Context matters in communication, and the world's email servers are basically funeral pyres for context.

There's an easy fix. Don't email when you're angry. Take a breath. Think. Write back when you're calm. You'll never regret it.

Oh, and if you take this next step before writing that email, you'll be glad you did it.

Know who you're communicating with and empathize with them.

No matter how clearly you think you have communicated, what people hear is not always what you say. Their own perspectives and moods and histories and diets and blood sugar and sleepless nights can all influence the meaning they take from your words. If you're aware of this, you'll have more empathy for anyone who misunderstands you, as opposed to being frustrated at how dumb everyone is.

Let's go back to the party for a moment, where it turns out that the person you were dying to talk to doesn't know that many people there. In fact, they didn't want anything but a night to unwind and indulge in some fun conversation after a long day. And this person definitely did not show up thinking, "Wow, I really wish someone would impress me!"

Now, if you knew all of this context before approaching, how might it change your approach?

Even though you can't know every detail about someone before you start getting to know them, there are assumptions that we can make. Plus, listening to people is never a bad thing. And not just listening, but what I call deep listening.

Deep listening isn't just hearing someone's words and paying just enough attention so that you can spot your cue to jump in and blab. Deep listening is more like tuning into a radio frequency so that the words and meaning coming through the speakers and flow clearly and effortlessly, impossible to misunderstand. Trying to come up with your next witty remark while listening with one ear is exhausting and often backfires. Truly listening leads to spontaneous satisfying communication, because then the person teaches you what they're like and how they prefer to be spoken to.

Let's take the context of deep listening back to the interview. Why do people hire other people? Because the company has an issue and they need someone to fix it. It's not because they would love to hear people rattling away from scripted material and telling unfalsifiable anecdotes about themselves. The day of an interviewer can be long, and nothing makes days feel longer than person after person walking in and saying the same thing because they think it's what you want to hear.

But if the interviewees took some time to think about what the company needed—to really empathize with the people running the company and conducting the interviews—they would improve their chances of getting the job and spare the recruiters a bunch of wasted time.

What about with the email? You're still seething about the audacity of that jerk who CC'd your boss, pointing out mistakes that weren't even yours. You're one step away from firing off a raging message and then poking a voodoo doll to teach the fool a lesson.

But here's what you don't know about the person who sent the email.

- She's going through a divorce.
- She's mad because you embarrassed her in a meeting yesterday without knowing it.
- She doesn't actually care about the task and when it's completed.

Now, there's no way for you to just know all of this, no matter how far back you step or how many deep, cleansing breaths you take. But you can always try to empathize with the person on the other end. You can ask yourself, "What might be going on with this person that would make their actions seem logical to them, even though they look like the height of stupidity and pettiness to me?"

Of course, it's always possible that the other person is just a jerk. It happens. But even in those cases, empathy still helps you. Every interaction where you choose the high road is a successful experiment in the laboratory of communication.

You can always empathize.

Now, for the words.

Speak the truth with compassion.

Commerce has turned communication into something of a technical game. Look at the advertising industry. How many products do exactly what their shrill marketing campaigns claim they do? Not enough. Look at the politicians. Either people have decided that it's more tolerable for their leaders to lie these days, or we're all just so burned out by the lying that we can barely muster the energy to care when they do.

Many think that good communication is about focusing on techniques, but technique isn't enough. You might be a gifted orator, but you'll never be as effective as when you also believe what you say, and you say what you believe to be true.

There are exceptions, maybe. The classic example is someone saying, "Does wearing this dress make me look fat?"

If the answer is yes, speaking the truth isn't very compassionate. There's probably a way to convey the answer in a different way, like, "I think it's great, but the yellow dress compliments your figure even better." That's compassion in practice.

Let's take one more trip back to the party. You're talking to this person you've been dying to meet and you're nervous. You're listening but you're still anxious.

What do you do? What do you say?

What if, instead of going into witty mode and laying it on thick as you rhapsodize your many accolades, you told the person the truth? That you were really interested in striking up a good conversation but you are a little nervous. What are the chances that person would be completely put off by your sincere and honest—and, possibly, endearing—vulnerability? Pretty slim.

This is "congruent communication." You said what was true and real for you. People don't respond as well to incongruent communication, and I think that at some level we all sense when it's happening.

Don't think of congruent communication as a way to seal the deal or get someone to like you. Just think of it as a favor you can do for yourself that will also incline others to respond to you favorably. If you express who you are, and the person isn't into it, you can simply file that under "good to know."

What about when the interviewer asks you a difficult question and suddenly all of your ideas about truth and compassion are put to the test in a higher-stakes situation? What if they say, "Why are you leaving your job? Don't you like your current employer?" and the truth is, you don't like your current employer and you don't get the respect you deserve. Should you say that?

Badmouthing a former or previous employer is always a red flag, and you recognize this. So, instead, you can honestly say, "I have appreciated my time with my current employer, but I do look forward to the respectful culture of (the interviewer's organization)." That gets your point across with skill and grace. They couldn't fault you for this. And if they looked ahead to the day when you might also leave their company, they would know that you would probably speak about them with the same level of professionalism and respect.

Now, back to the angry email. You know that you shouldn't respond angrily. But should you forget it entirely? Being compassionate doesn't mean being a doormat or a pushover. It doesn't mean that you shouldn't stand up for yourself or that you should automatically assume you're in the wrong or that you shouldn't make waves under any circumstances. If you really have something to say in response, do it firmly but compassionately. It might be even more compassionate to request some personal time with the person to have a face-to-face talk.

These three examples all show that *how* you say something can be as important—more, in some cases—than *what* you say. And once you've said what you have to say, the way that you listen and receive the feedback sets the tone for everything that comes next in your relationship with the person in front of you.

We're not dealing with an object like a computer that will give us a certain output every time if we can just push the right button. We are interacting with other people. Other people require compassion, concern, focus, and our best intentions. Even then, things can still go wrong, but at the very least, *how* we say things is always in our control.

Key Lesson: *Speak the truth with compassion.*

Key Points:
- *Communication starts with your state.*
- *Know who you're communicating with and empathize with them.*
- *Speak the truth with compassion.*

Action Steps for Learning

Action 1: Learn Small Talk

This advice is not for the social, extroverted folks who already love small talk. This is for the introverts who find themselves surrounded by strangers at a party. There is a method to conversation that can be learned. There are plenty of books and YouTube videos out there. Pick a method that works for you. Practice. Use it as a script. Over time, you will be comfortable striking up a conversation with anyone.

Action 2: Learn Improv

Let's face it. Typing comments into a text box on social media is doing nothing to help your communication skills. What is the opposite of that? Speaking extemporaneously in front of another human being. A big challenge, but it will make you a much better communicator. There are plenty of improv classes held all over the country. Sign up!

Action 3: Handling Difficult Conversations

It's easy to chat with people you know about things you enjoy talking about. It's hard to have the difficult conversations with, let's say a colleague who isn't doing his or her share of the work. Yet, these difficult conversations will make or break your relationships and career. Learn how to navigate these conversations. There are plenty of books out there about the subject. (e.g. *Crucial Conversations*) Read about it and understand the process. Then have those difficult conversations.

Notes on Other Actions

What other actions could you take?

Word Problems: Communication = ?

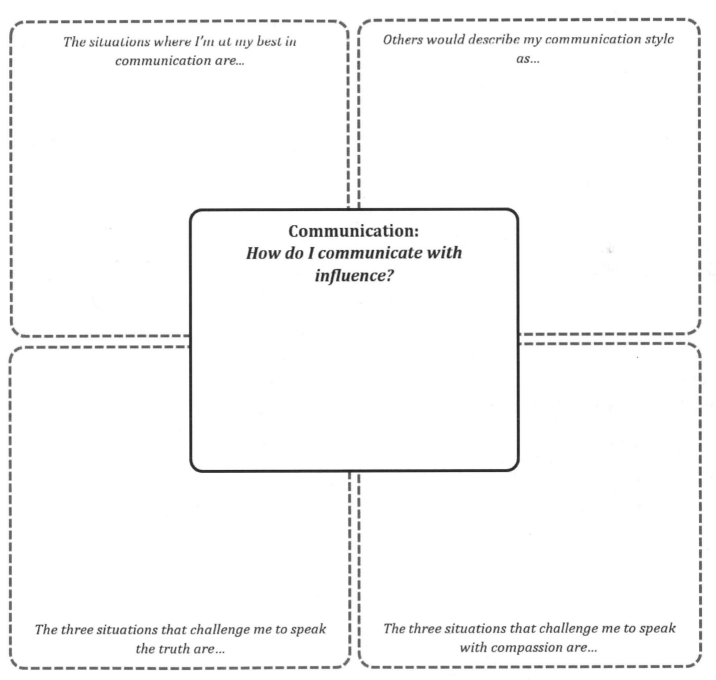

The situations where I'm at my best in communication are...

Others would describe my communication style as...

**Communication:
*How do I communicate with influence?***

The three situations that challenge me to speak the truth are...

The three situations that challenge me to speak with compassion are...

Developing Your Unique Formula: the COMMUNITY Domain

NETWORK

Question 5: *What kind of people do I need to know?*

> *The answer to this question is explored in the NETWORK chapter.*

+

RELATION-SHIPS

Question 6: *What is my way to build connection with others?*

> *The answer to this question is explored in the RELATIONSHIPS chapter.*

+

COMMUNICA-TION

Question 7: *How do I communicate with influence?*

> *The answer to this question is explored in the COMMUNICATION chapter.*

=

COMMUNITY

Question 8: *How will I show up for others?*

> *Recommendation: Answer this question after you have answered questions 5 to 7, as a synthesis of the answers from those supporting questions.*

DOMAIN:
PURPOSE

- - - - - - - - - - - - -

HOW WILL I CONTRIBUTE TO THE WORLD AROUND ME?

I am of the opinion that my life belongs to the community, and as long as I live, it is my privilege to do for it whatever I can. I want to be thoroughly used up when I die, for the harder I work, the more I live. Life is no 'brief candle' to me. It is a sort of splendid torch which I have got hold of for a moment, and I want to make it burn as brightly as possible before handing it on to the future generations.

~ GEORGE BERNARD SHAW

How will I contribute to the world around me?

Contributing vs Consuming: Be a 'Giver' Instead of a 'Taker'

Driving home from work one day, I was listening to a radio show. An elderly woman was reflecting on her life and noted that she really loved eating chicken. In fact, after doing a quick calculation, she estimated that she had eaten between 7,000 and 10,000 chickens during her lifetime and then wondered aloud, "Was my one life worth the lives of 10,000 chickens?"

Although we work hard and often feel self-made, it's important to remember that our being alive comes at a "cost" to the world. According to the Environmental Protection Agency, in 2014 the average American produced 1,606 lbs. of trash[22], the average American driver consumed roughly 650 gallons of gasoline[23], and the U.S. generated around 50 lbs. of e-waste per capita in 2014[24]. Have you ever wondered what happens when we replace our phones every few years?

It's quite the cost, so doesn't it make sense that we are wired to want to give back to the world that is giving to us?

But do we? How well are you contributing back? Are YOU worth all those chickens?

I once asked a doctor about his ultimate goal and was stunned by his response. He could have said "curing cancer" or "alleviating suffering" or any number of things, lofty and prosaic. Instead, he said, "I want to play golf all day."

Okay, imagine that you love golf enough to play it all day. Maybe you already do. But does this really make you happy in a lasting, satisfying way? Is a life of nothing but golf a life well-lived?

Most of us would not answer that our purpose is as self-serving as playing golf all day because ours tend to play out in more subtle ways disguised as practicality. We say things like, "I need to get good grades in order to get a good job." If you dive deeper into this statement, you will see that the person is focused on personal performance in school in order to further personal security. All self-serving motives. Not bad, just self-serving.

We are living in a very abundant time. We have more material wealth now than at any other time in human history. We CAN play a lot of golf. We CAN eat a lot of chickens. Yet for all this material wealth and all this consumption, are we actually any happier as a result?

So if consumption and a self-serving focus doesn't lead to happiness, what does? Meaning and community do. And Purpose. We all need to contribute towards something that is greater than and beyond ourselves to experience true fulfillment.

In the Army, soldiers must often risk their lives in battle. Would they do that because of the meager pay? Yummy rations? No. They risk their lives for their sense of personal integrity (meaning), for their comrades (community), and for defense of the nation (purpose). If soldiers were focused mainly on self-preservation and comfort, they would never be able to summon the courage it takes to be a good solider.

But what about you? When will you be at YOUR best and summon the most courage, effort, and dedication? It's when you can align yourself with YOUR meaning, community, and purpose. In this domain, we will be exploring the concept of purpose. It is about your commitment and contribution to something greater.[25]

Meaning ↓ Community ↖

To contribute your unique gift, while finding belonging in a caring community, to something meaningful that is greater than yourself.

Purpose ↖

So, here's something you may never have asked yourself: Will you be a "giver," focused on your contribution, or will you be a "taker," focused on your consumption? And if you're going to work, to study, to live life, what will be the purpose of all of that? How will you contribute to the world around you?

Why are you unhappy? Because 99.9 percent of everything you think, and of everything you do, is for yourself—and there isn't one. ~ Wei Wu Wei

Domain: Purpose

Can you answer the question: *How will I contribute to the world around me?*

We're not talking about grandiose causes where you single-handedly solve an intractable problem of society and save the whales, cure cancers, end racism, or fight world hunger. We're talking about finding an issue or cause that is meaningful to you and taking some initial steps to contribute to it in your own way. In time, the body of your contribution may indeed be transformative, and you will be able to look back at your life and career and be proud of what you have done. Before you can answer this question, consider the three "variables" below. These "variables" (mission, vision, process are fundamental pieces of this larger question of how you will contribute.

Variables: Mission, Vision, Process

Mission: *What am I committed to that is greater than myself?* (Variable 7)

Random effort produces random results, so we're going to help you consider what you should be working on. Once you know that, you'll be able to focus your efforts on contributing towards something that is meaningful to you in a way that is suited to your strengths and values.

Vision: *How will I define success?* (Variable 8)

Before a skyscraper was a skyscraper, it was a vision, and then it was a plan. Before a company was a company, it was a vision, and then it was a plan. Look at any "thing;" before that "thing" was a "thing," it was a vision. In our lives, when we can "see" something, we can take steps to make it a reality. Visions drive our actions. For your life and for your career, what is the vision? Developing the vision will allow you to plan and to take actions to making the vision a reality.

Process: *What is my next step?* (Variable 9)

In the chapters on mission and vision, we plot a direction for our lives and set out to plan the steps. In that plan, we often want to know every step in between. We want that certainty. However, our lives are not that linear. We can't control the external events that will happen three years from now. What we can control is the actions we take now—the next step. My mentor would use the analogy of building the bridge as you cross it. In taking each "next step" with intention and courage, we build the habits which create our habits and destiny.

The next three chapters are about "mission," "vision," and "process"— the variables that will help you answer the question of how you will contribute.

DOMAIN: PURPOSE
Variable 7 =
MISSION

- - - - - - - - - - -

WHAT AM I COMMITTED TO THAT IS GREATER THAN MYSELF?

I slept and dreamt that life was joy. I awoke and saw that life was service. I acted and behold, service was joy.

~ RABINDRANATH TAGORE

What am I committed to that is greater than myself?

"If you look at your career, what do you really, *really* want from it?" I posed this question to my class of post-residency doctors.

"To play as much golf as possible!" chimed Mitch, a short, energetic guy with an assertive presence and sharp wit.

Oh great, I thought to myself. *There's always one of these opinions in every class. If you think about it though, it does have some logic to it. If you like playing golf, then why not just play golf all the time?*

"Mitch, just to be clear, are you one of those people whose life-long dream was to become a golfer, but then your parents pressured you into going to med school?" I asked, tempering my sarcasm.

Mitch grinned from ear to ear. "No, I just enjoy playing golf. It's a lot more enjoyable than work on many days."

"Yes, I can see what you mean. Sometimes, I just want to play golf too!" I said only half-jokingly.

Everyone has those days.

I paused to gather my thoughts before continuing my line of inquiry, "Let's do a bit of a thought experiment. Pretend that you are eighty-five years old and looking back at your life. If you played golf forty hours a week for the duration of your career, would you be happy with yourself?"

"Well, of course not," he quipped. "I like ice cream too, but that doesn't mean that my purpose is to ingest 10,000 gallons of it."

"I wonder what your eighty-five-year-old YOU would want you to do with your career? What would be success in *his* eyes?" I pressed.

"I want to help others who have struggled with stomach issues…" He started and continued to share that when he was younger, his stomach problems would incapacitate him on many days. When he went to the doctor, they couldn't do that much for him. In fact, his problem was never really "solved," although it did get better as he got older.

"Today, as a GI (stomach) doctor, I am researching irritable bowel syndrome and have plans to open a new clinic to help teenagers with stomach conditions." The sarcastic tone was long-gone from his voice, all of his energy now focused on his mission.

"What is more important and meaningful—what you just described, or playing a million rounds of golf?" It was a rhetorical question of course—one he didn't have to answer. He knew his own answer, and the rest of the class sighed as they all collectively remembered the reason they got into medicine.

They were all deep in thought when Mitch's wit disrupted the class again. "I wonder if I could set up a clinic—the first of its kind in the world—where I can see patients on the golf course, and we can play a couple of holes together."

"And eat a gallon of ice cream!" another student shouted.

Man, I love my job, I thought as I waited for the laughter to settle.

We all have a certain responsibility for action that gives the meaning to our lives, and it's not unusual to find that it stems from a personal story that means something to us.

That's why this book is written. This is part of *my purpose.* And I am passionate about it because of the experience I had in college. What I am offering to university students through this book is exactly what I wished I'd had while I was there the first time through it.

So, how do you actually figure out your purpose? How can a privileged person—and make no mistake, if you're reading this, you're on one of the top rungs on the global the ladder of privilege—find a sense of mission?

Maybe it's because I'm a business guy, but I find that it's easiest to demonstrate this concept of purpose through a story of an actual business that succeeded.

An Analogy...

In 1995, in the early stages of the internet, Pierre Omidyar was looking to create an online marketplace (which eventually became eBay). At the time, much of the power in markets were in the hands of brokers or intermediaries. "Regular people" did not have access. So the marketplace he was looking to build would be inclusive of as many "regular people" as possible, and it would leverage a larger group of people to participate in the exchange and contribution of the marketplace. When eBay was nothing but a concept in its founder's mind, it might have worked like this.

First, he defined a large, significant set of **people**. It's rare that a target group can encompass everyone, but eBay was able to include nearly everyone with an internet connection.[26]

Next, he defined a **problem** that he thought he could help people solve. The problems of eBay users are not high stakes in the way that Bill Gates's philanthropic work is, but eBay's buyers and sellers still had problems and needs. The sellers were everyone, from people with cluttered houses looking to make a few extra bucks to savvy resellers who saw an opportunity to use eBay for steady, massive revenue streams. Their big problem, prior to eBay, was that their potential buyers were limited to geography. Not everyone in the country can come to your yard sale. Anyone in the world with access to a computer can come to your global auction on eBay.[27]

After targeting the group and identifying the problem he wanted to solve, he had to create an **approach**. How would eBay solve the problems of its buyers and sellers?

Honestly, it never should have worked. Early critics of eBay basically said, "Here's how it's going to work. I'll send you junk and you'll send me a check that bounces." But of course's, that's not what happened. Through a system of social feedback and rating, buyers and sellers who otherwise had very little basis of trust could conduct transactions with relative confidence. [28]

The People, Problem, and Approach schema applies to you as well. Think about it. Whether your reach is large or not, you're at the middle of a circle of influence. You're able to affect other people, because other people are in your life.

The people around you are upset about something. They each have pain and some sort of void. So, you think about them and their pain, and you do it carefully. How much pain do they have? What would it look like if it were resolved? Can it be lessened? What would it take to get there?

Then you address the problem in a way that only you can, using your strengths. In the beginning, you don't even have to have any particular expertise to make this happen. You don't need to be a statistics wizard or stumble onto the creation of penicillin. You just have to be willing to think, and to act. If a person needs to hear a kind word, it makes little difference whether it comes from you or me. We're each uniquely differentiated in our ability to help, even if we say the same words to the same person.

We exist to serve others. (PEOPLE : Problem : Approach)

If you look at our human existence, on the one hand, we are individuals. We have a body. We have a name. We have our customized cell phone ringtones. At the same time, we are also a part of something larger than ourselves. We have a family. We have a school or professional community. We have our society. These "systems" of people require that the members of the system contribute in some way for the overall well-functioning of the system.

If I'm on a basketball team, and I'm point guard, then I have to dribble and pass. If I were the center, I would have to defend the area around the basket and rebound. We all have to contribute in some coordinated way, otherwise the system/team doesn't work.

Even as individuals, we are also a system. We have organs which are made up of cells. We rely on the members of our system (our heart, lungs, cells) to perform and contribute for our continued existence. Imagine that you're a red blood cell. What would be your "mission"? Your mission is to deliver oxygen to the tissue of the body. What if you, as the red blood cell, said, "Nah, I'm not going to deliver oxygen. I'm just going to sit around and consume energy." Then of course, you'd be cancer.

So we are individuals. AND we are part of larger systems. AND we are ourselves a system consisting of yet smaller systems. Weird, right? It seems that the larger systems rely on the function and contribution of its members to work properly. When society holds up "service to others" as a desired ideal, it is not because of mushy sentimentality. Society actually does need its members to contribute.

Our purpose **IS** this contribution.

The only challenge is that, unlike a blood cell whose function is hard-wired, we get to choose. That's great! But…that stinks, because how we should contribute is not clear to us. It takes time for us to live our life and to reflect for this vision of how we're going to contribute to come into focus. Also, we're unique. So while we can partially model ourselves on people who are similar to us, there's a part of the journey that only we can access.

Let's return to our analogy with building a business and using that for our own reflective process.

So, what about official organizations? Their purpose is to provide goods and services, *not* solely to make money. Whether they fulfill their missions or not, the fact that most companies and non-profits have mission statements is evidence that they pay, at the very least, lip service to the idea.

Have you ever flown on Southwest? Here's how they justify their existence:

> *To connect people to what's important in their lives through friendly, reliable, and low-cost air travel.* [29]

Now, gripe all you want about leg room and the paltry size of the peanut bags, Southwest is shooting big. The company exists to connect people to what's important to them. Hard to argue with that.

Microsoft wants you to know that its purpose is:

> *To empower every person and every organization on the planet to achieve more.* [30]

Is that what you think of when you boot up a PC? Probably not. But it's what Bill Gates thought about when creating his company.

Teach For America:

> Expanding opportunity for children by affecting profound systemic change. We find, develop, and support a diverse network of leaders from classrooms, schools, and every sector and field in order to shape the broader system in which schools operate.[31]

What about a hospital? They may phrase it differently, but every hospital shares a mission: promoting the health of the community.

YOU can define your purpose as clearly as any company.

PEOPLE: Who are the people whom you will impact?

Let's drill down into the process of selecting the people you most want to help, or the group you think you can benefit the most.

Who will be the most affected by your work? Writers are often encouraged to write with their ideal audience in mind. Who's the ideal audience for your efforts?

Next, describe the group of people in as much detail as you can. Ideally, it's a large group, so be realistic, but try to describe everyone who fits into the niche in which you are working.

Now, just to make yourself stretch, add three to four more groups. Try to see if you can set them apart from the large group you already targeted. This isn't to say that your group, approach, and ideas won't evolve over time. But the longer you can stay focused, once you have made decisions based on the steps outlined above, the more progress you will make.

People	Description of People (Group)

All problems are not the same. (People : PROBLEM : Approach)

There are lots of problems in the world. There are plenty that you could tackle, but how do you know *exactly* what to work on?

In the old days of guilds, feudalism, and other structures, this issue of what problem one would address was mostly "assigned" by tradition or your station in life. If your father was the town baker, you were probably going to spend your life kneading dough. If he was a blue-blooded aristocrat, you were headed for a life of pomp, propriety, and potential ceremonial diplomatic roles.

Today, it's almost an understatement to say that people have an abundance of choices. On its face, this looks like a good thing. I mean, what would be the downside? Isn't more choice better? Of course, and if you've ever had to make a choice about which salad dressing you should buy or which show to watch on Netflix, you know the answer is not as straightforward as it seems.

How do we navigate these choices?

If you look at your life, there are clues. Why did certain things happen in your past? What were the consequences? How did those things shape what you "care about," or how did they shape your values?

For Mitch, the GI (gastrointestinal) doctor, he could have become any type of doctor. Why did he choose GI? Because of his experience as a teen with GI problems and the values that emerged from that experience, it was a meaningful medical specialty for him.

Our lives have imprinted us in some way. If you look closely, you will find the traces of that imprint influencing your life through your values. Maybe you grew up with very little money, and now you value financial security. Maybe you always loved stories as a kid, and now you want to write stories for others.

For me, I lacked a meaningful experience in college. That was very important to me and I didn't get it. Everything eventually led me to a desire to go back and "fix" college. I wanted to make college—or at least, higher education—something that students would more meaningfully engage with, thereby appreciating it more and turning it into a value.

I think life gives you clues about what you should be doing through this imprinting process and your emerging values. So, if you reflect on your life, and then clarify and follow those values, you "fulfill" your purpose—making you "whole." The amazing aspect of this is that what you think you are doing to serve others, you are also doing for yourself.

So, what issues do you want to work on? You don't want to just "do anything," or "do stuff," or "make money." There has to be more than simply staying in motion, punching a clock, and collecting a check. You can do all of those things and stay fulfilled, happy, and eager to report to work, as long as those things are part of you acting according to your purpose and values.

PROBLEM: Which problems do you feel compelled to do something about?

Think about the problems you are most engaged with fixing. Write a description of the problem to further clarify the scope of the problem. Consider how "painful" the problem is to those it affects. The more "pain," the greater the urgency for someone (perhaps you) to work on it. Try to assign each of them a position on a scale of 1 (meh) – 10 (urgent) in terms of how much it "pulls on you."

Problem	Description of Problem

We each have something unique to contribute. (People : Problem : APPROACH)

Once a problem is defined, there are different ways to solve it. For the sake of simplicity, here are four general approaches

- Generate a novel idea – Think about Steve Jobs and Elon Musk. Their ideas have been *so* novel that it appears as if they never have any thoughts that are normal or mundane. Those ideas led to the iPhone and may very well produce the first manned space flight to Mars.

- Organize people – You need people to help you execute an idea. And not just people, but the *right* people. There is perhaps no better example of this than Oprah. Her net worth is in direct proportion to her ability to create a massive army of people who evangelize her message.

- Develop process – Without a plan, it's going to be tough to produce the results you want. Henry Ford's idea for the automobile wouldn't have worked as well if he hadn't come up with the process for the auto factories that made mass production a reality.

- Execute / Compete – Plans, regardless of who comes up with them have to be put in motion, and if you can do it single-mindedly with a competitive spirit, you're way ahead of the curve. A person like Jeff Bezos from Amazon is a master of relentless execution, combined with almost pathological competitiveness. I'm not saying that's going to be your ideal mindset, but it's hard to argue with his results.

Which approach should *you* take? Think back to your strengths. There are approaches which are "natural" to you. What have you noticed about yourself? How do you tend to "handle things"? (I have adapted this from my mentor's Competing Values Model.[32])

- Form a coalition...
- Develop a community...
- Teach and educate...
- Support and develop...
- Promote a culture...
- Empower a group...
- Build awareness...

- Discover a new method...
- Design a new product...
- Found an organization...
- Transform existing methods...
- Create a new program...
- Open a new practice...
- Experiment...

- Gather and provide information...
- Analyze data for insight...
- Develop measurement...
- Standardize a process...
- Organize a system...
- Develop policy...
- Manage a complex effort...

- Run an organization...
- Achieve goals...
- Enable decision...
- Initiate action...
- Respond to crises/challenge...
- Implement a policy...
- Orchestrate a campaign...

APPROACH: How do you naturally tend to handle problems?

Think about the approaches which are more "natural" to you. If it's helpful, look at the color wheel and select actions which describe how you tend to handle problems and be "generally helpful" to others. Write that approach in the table below. Further write a description of the approach which is customized to you.

Approach	Description of Approach

Key Lesson: Define your purpose.

Key Points:

- *We exist to serve others.*
- *All problems are not the same.*
- *We each have something unique to contribute.*

Your mission...if you choose to accept it. (PEOPLE : PROBLEM : APPROACH)

Let's now write you mission statement using the People, Problem, Approach method.

- Go to the **People** section of this chapter, where you identified three to five groups of people that you hope to impact. Select one of the groups. Write that group below in the "People" row.

- Go to the **Problem** section of this chapter, where you identified three to five problems that you hope to impact. Select one of the problems. Write that problem below in the "Problem" row.

- Go to the **Approach** section of this chapter, where you identified three to five approaches that you use to solve problems. Select one of the approaches. Write that approach below in the "Approach" row.

- Put it all together. "My purpose is to help (people) with a (problem) through (approach)." That's it!

My Purpose:

(People)	To help...	
(Problem)	with...	
(Approach)	through...	

Don't' worry, this was just an exercise. You can continue to change and shape this statement as you engage new people and problems and expressions of your purpose through experimentation.

Action Steps for Learning

Action 1: Five Years to Live

You found out that you only had five years to live. (*Gulp.*) You can't put off your dreams any more. You must start the process to realize your dreams today. What would you be building towards with your last five years staring you in the face?

Action 2: Volunteer for Something You Care About

I'm not talking about volunteering in order to have it on your resume. I'm talking about the type of volunteering where you are doing it because you believe fully in the cause. If you're ever stuck wondering about what your "cause" is, go out there and volunteer. That is a powerful way to awaken your purpose.

Action 3: Just Ask Yourself

Take about twenty to thirty minutes by yourself and ask, "What is my authentic purpose in life?" Then, just start writing down the answers that come to your mind. For every answer you write down, you will feel the emotional charge of that statement. Some will have more, some less. Just keep writing. At some point, you will write something that will have such a high charge that you will begin to cry. That's the one you've been waiting for.

Notes on Other Actions

What other actions could you take?

Word Problems: Mission = ?

The people who most need what I have to contribute are...

The problems I feel most compelled to address are...

Mission:
What am I committed to that is greater than myself?

If I had $100 million in the bank, and money was not an issue, it would be meaningful for me to do...

The ways I can best contribute towards solving a problem are...

DOMAIN: PURPOSE
Variable 8 =
VISION

- - - - - - - - - - - - - -

HOW WILL I DEFINE SUCCESS?

*A vision is not just a picture of what could
be; it is an appeal to our better selves,
a call to become something more.*

~ROSABETH MOSS KANTER

How will I define success?

Four first-year med students walked into my office and sat down to chat about their first semester of school. In just a few minutes of conversation, I knew they were doing well on their exams and earning good grades, but their worried expressions told me something else was going on.

"So, what else are you feeling at this point in your education?" I probed.

They all shot each other a quick glance, nodding at the young woman who looked eager to respond. "Well, we've all been talking about how hard we are working, and how we don't want to miss out on our lives while we are working at this goal…"

She looked at her peers, who quickly chimed in with their observations and feelings. They saw that some of their classmates were studying day in and day out—fourteen hours a day including class—while others were barely studying at all. They were going on hikes and riding their mountain bikes and posting gorgeous pictures of themselves in nature on the class Facebook account for all to see.

One of the young men summed up the tension in a few words. "Most of us are from out of state, and we want to enjoy the benefits of being in a medical school in Utah. Wouldn't it be a shame to study our lives away?" He paused and cocked his head to one side. "On the other hand, it seems irresponsible to not study. After all, we are soon going to be doctors, and in order to be as prepared as we can to take care of patients, we need to be diligent in our studies, right?"

Wow. They genuinely feel paralyzed by these two options.

I smiled at this earnest group of students and asked, "What would it take for you to say that you had properly enjoyed what this beautiful place has to offer?"

Every eye in the room lit up, as they realized the power of this simple question. They had allowed this vague uneasiness that they might misspend their time to nearly rob them of a unique experience.

"Well," the first young woman who had spoken jumped in again, "I want to visit the national parks…"

"Yes, they are beautiful indeed. How often do you want to enjoy them?"

After a bit of discussion, they settled on visiting two national parks every three months so that by the end of the year, they would have visited the national park eight times. They agreed that that if they did this, that would mean that they had properly enjoyed the state. No longer would they have the nagging anxiety every time they saw a classmate on Facebook riding their mountain bike.

A little reflection often translates uncertainty into one's own defined intention, I thought as I watched them leave my office a little lighter and happier than they had walked in.

Medical schools are generally filled with Type A, high-performing, ambitious people. They all want badly to succeed, and to distinguish themselves. Most of them think that they must be at or toward the top of their class in terms of test performance to be considered successful. Given the culture, it's not hard to see how this develops. But this is success defined and dictated by external social forces, not from an authentic inner criteria.

Not everybody gets to be top of the class, but everyone can be successful and excellent on their own terms, provided they're willing to think about what those terms may be.

Parkinson's Law

In 1955, a British naval historian by the name of Cyril Parkinson penned an adage in *The Economist* that became known as Parkinson's Law. "Work expands so as to fill the time available for its completion." [33]

Whatever your situation may be, Parkinson's Law is alive and well in our lives today, and not to our benefit. Have you ever had a meeting that was one hour long, and then it took one hour just to talk about what was going to be on the agenda? Or one of the meetings where someone scheduled it for two hours and the only reason it seems to last for two hours is because someone scheduled it for two hours? A meeting for the sake of a meeting? What about later when you go to a meeting that only takes thirty minutes and the same amount of work was accomplished as in the one-hour agenda-reading marathon?

What exactly is filling our lives? What is expanding uselessly into the spaces you could (should) claim as your own, clogging up the channels that could be used to improve your life? Yes, we're busy, but many of the things that make us so insanely busy aren't necessary at all. Is that really a reality any of us want to be confronting when we're down to our last bucket of days?

A Roman philosopher named Seneca wrote an essay titled, *On the Shortness of Life*. Of the many gems from the piece, this one might be the best:

> *It is not that we have so little time but that we lose so much... The life we receive is not short but we make it so; we are not ill provided but we use what we have wastefully.*

When you lose something, you try to retrace your steps and remember the last place you had it. You can't, however, retrace your steps to find lost time.

If we're honest, we'll most likely find that boredom drives us more than purpose. How much time do we spend looking at social media? Surfing the Internet? Playing video games? Watching TV? How many of those activities are purposeful and intentional? So when people say, "I don't have time to do something," is it really that there's not enough time? The most effective people I know tend to be the ones who always know how to free up their schedules.

Here's a corollary to Parkinson's Law:

> If you're not engaged in purposeful activities, your time will be filled by distractions.

So how do we avoid that?

Begin with the end in mind.

Towards the end of his life, my dad often lamented not having spent more time with me and my brother. (Our family owned Chinese restaurants which took him out of the family picture much of the time.) He tried hard to fulfill his role as a father, but things didn't turn out how he had intended. He certainly isn't the first person who looked back on his life and realized that the path had wound its way through territory that was surprising, and often baffling.

Now that I'm a father, I have a better understanding of him. It's easier to have empathy, compassion, and gratitude for his efforts. I have three sons. The thought of them removing me from a family picture is unbearable. And it's precisely because of the time I've spent reflecting on my father's life that I've got a clear vision of how to make sure that never happens.

What I wanted was to have a meaningful relationship with each of my sons, so that when I look back in my life I have no regrets. That was the decision I made: to put in the time and effort to make it happen. It's simple, but not simplistic. In order to figure out this vision, I had to decide what "meaningful" even meant to me, and what I hoped it would eventually mean for my sons.

I know myself pretty well. My schedule is highly regimented and probably always will be. This means that I know in advance that I have a certain amount of time that I can devote to my kids. And I don't have as much time with them as my wife, Angie. To make the most of the time that I do have, I have to have a strategy.

My oldest, Nate, loves to play baseball. When he was eight, a teacher asked him, "What you want to be when you grow up?"

"A baseball player."

"So you want to be a baseball player. Is that right?"

"I don't WANT to be a baseball player. I WILL be a baseball player."

When it came to Nate and baseball, I decided that I would always try my best to play baseball with him whenever he wanted to play baseball. There's certainly more to being a dad, but it made sense to me to prioritize what he cares about most. When Nate is forty years old and people ask him to describe his dad, I want him to say, "My dad always took the time to play baseball with me."

In his influential book *The 7 Habits of Highly Effective People*, Stephen R. Covey suggests, along similar lines, that we "begin with the end in mind." For me, this could mean picturing the day of my funeral. What would I want people to say as they spoke about their memories of me?

In knowing what I want, I can take the steps necessary to turn my wishes into reality.

When you set your own agenda and work towards it, you can become a force of nature. Most people follow the agenda set by society, the company, peer pressure, tradition or their boss, and then wonder why it's so hard to find their unique excellence and to live a life that honors their gifts and talents.

So, let's talk process.

Here are some categories to describe the (eight) domains of life:

Career, Family, Financial, Health, Learning, Leisure, Religious / Spiritual, Social

Interpretations may vary on a couple of these, but hopefully you have an idea of what each domain connotes for you.

Balance across the eight domains is critical. Often, people will have very strong intentions in certain domains like career while neglecting others, like family. When neglected, these facets of the wheel fall into states of disrepair, and eventually they'll drag your attention away from what your strongest intentions. It's not hard to see how this could happen. We all have talents and temperaments that skew us towards some domains more than others. But when you put too much emphasis on one, the others suffer accordingly. Eventually, this will catch up to you. It's happening beneath the surface, even if the short-term returns appear positive.

Here are some questions that would help you consider the eight domains as a path to your goal.

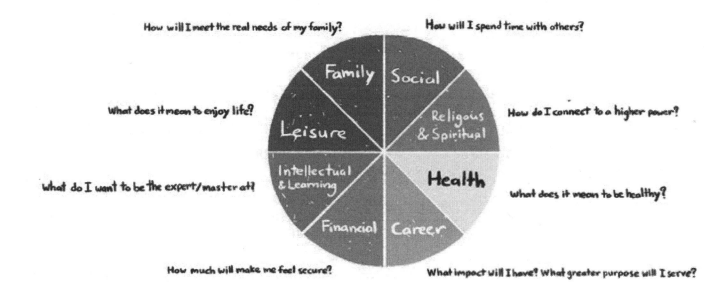

If you can answer these questions, your agenda will write itself for you. It will glow with clarity and you won't be able to ignore it, no matter what diversions shriek for your intention. (Please refer to the worksheet "Defining Your Agenda" at the end of this section.)

You're not doing it wrong if it's hard to answer the questions. Maybe your inner voice isn't fully developed yet. Maybe social and family obligations are still influencing your answers.

I want you to ignore them and go talk to a coach. This coach always knows what is best for you. But which coach? It is YOU when you are eighty-five years old. This coach has been through everything and can give you the right advice for the questions that you're facing now. Listen to his answers. He is nearly at the end, and he is the perfect guide to help you begin with the end in mind.

Once you have answered the questions regarding the eight domains, you are ready to begin setting goals.

This isn't to say that you can't make use of prompts, particularly in the beginning. One exercise that I highly recommend comes from a development group by the name of Jim Rohn. It's called the fifty goals exercise. (Please refer to the worksheet "50 Goals" at the end of this section.) Here's how it works.

Find a quiet place. Begin brainstorming some goals for each of the eight domains. For example, in the health domain, perhaps you've always wanted to run a marathon. I had a colleague who had a goal of watching a baseball game in every major league baseball park with his son. Perhaps you've always wanted to get a PhD. For me, I've always wanted to own a business.

Take enough time to do it right. Ponder your ideas in each domain. Listen to yourself and don't judge.

Then, write down as many of your goals as you can. See if the eight domains are equally represented, more or less. Some of these goals seem far away. They might as well be on the moon for how distant and hazy they are. But you'll hit some of them in a much shorter time. Organize your goals so that you can see every aspiration, spanning every time frame, and look at them all in the same place.

Think about this year. Come up with one to three things that, having been achieved, would make this year a successful year for you? Now start weighing your actions and decisions against those things. Simple. Not easy, but simple.

Okay, now let's zoom out with a wider lens. What will you have done ten years from now?

Push beyond your comfort zone.

On September 12, 1962, Pres. John F. Kennedy delivered a speech at Rice University to announce the intention of putting a person on the moon. Up to that point, the Soviet Union was winning the potential arms race of space exploration. Kennedy said that the United States would land a person on the moon and bring them safely back to earth by the end of the decade of the 60s. What an audacious claim! There were metals that needed to be invented to make the moon landing possible that hadn't even been thought of yet, let alone invented!

What Kennedy did not say was: "We'll try harder in the space race and hopefully we'll land a person on the moon and if not will develop another plan, so yeah, you know, whatever, hopefully it'll go our way."

He said it. It happened. This is the power of a bold vision.

You'll never grow as much as when you are the most challenged, so pick challenging goals. Not implausible, not impossible, but goals that will really make you stretch. Thoreau understood this when he said:

> *We must walk consciously only part way towards our goal and then leap into the dark to our success.*

Kennedy threw down a gauntlet and insisted that the nation strive towards that monumental achievement. He basically said, I defy you to show me that we can't do it. He challenged the nation to achieve something that it didn't know it could do.

Consider a bit of trepidation and anxiety to be clues about the goals that might have the biggest payoff. Doubts are essential to progress. If no one is doubting, no one is wondering. If no one is wondering, no one is asking. If no one is asking, where are the answers supposed to come from?

Let go of the idea that you'll be able to see all the way to the end of your biggest goals. Embrace the struggle and uncertainty and then hurl yourself joyfully into your intentions.

In 2015, my wife and I were considering future career options. I had been teaching a class on leadership, in which I had students write create personal mission statements. I had an idea for my wife and me.

Why don't we write down our mission statements and email them back to each other every day?

This might seem a sick kind of fun, but we all need something to keep us off the streets, yes? Angie was skeptical but agreed to humor me. At a professional conference shortly after we started doing this, she was approached by someone who wanted her to become a department chair at the University of Utah. Had we been job hunting, Utah would not have been a high-priority destination on our shortlist. However, we looked at the jobs that they were offering us and were shocked to find that both jobs fit our mission statement perfectly. In fact, perhaps Utah was the *only* place that had the jobs that could have satisfied both our mission criteria.

Things like this have happened to me constantly since I started applying these methods, and I have learned to trust the process. I know that I am responsible for the *WHAT* and the *WHY*, but the *HOW* is something that is often resolved in ways beyond my understanding.

Despite not needing to know the *HOW*, goals should be concrete. Here's an easy acronym to memorize. SMART.

The S stands for specific, something that you can see and touch, not something abstract.

The M stands for measurable, numbers, how big, how many?

The A stands for attainable, but a stretch.

The R stands for relevant, something that people care about.

The T stands for time bound, by a certain time.

Now, take one of your goals from the fifty goals exercise that means a lot to you. Expand that goal into something that is written in the SMART format. (Please refer to the worksheet "SMART Goals" at the end of this section.)

Don't forget, you're probably going to meet that eighty-five-year-old version of you one day, but that doesn't mean you can't access that person's wisdom today.

And that coach is going to tell you to be bold, be aggressive, be joyful, and to live in a way that you'll never have to regret. This is the process of becoming who you should be, by doing what you should do.

> **Key Lesson:** *Set a goal and work towards it.*
>
> **Key Points:**
> - *Work expands so as to fill the time available for its completion (Parkinson's Law).*
> - *Begin with the end in mind.*
> - *Push beyond your comfort zone.*

Worksheet: Defining Your Agenda

Career	*What impact will you have? What greater purpose will you serve?*
Family	*How will you meet the "real" needs of your family?*
Financial	*How much will make you feel secure?*
Health	*What does it mean to be healthy?*
Learning	*What do you want to be the expert/master at?*
Leisure	*What does it mean to enjoy life?*
Religious / Spiritual	*How do you connect to a higher power?*
Social	*How will you spend time with others?*

Worksheet: 50 Goals

1		26	
2		27	
3		28	
4		29	
5		30	
6		31	
7		32	
8		33	
9		34	
10		35	
11		36	
12		37	
13		38	
14		39	
15		40	
16		41	
17		42	
18		43	
19		44	
20		45	
21		46	
22		47	
23		48	
24		49	
25		50	

Worksheet: SMART Goals

Specific   *Something you can see and touch (not abstract).*

Measurable   *Numbers. How big? How many?*

Attainable   *Attainable, but a stretch. 50% unknown.*

Relevant   *Solving something that people care about.*

Time-Bound   *By a certain time.*

In the space below, write a goal statement for yourself or your organization you lead using the "SMART" format.

> **By _____, I am committed to...**
>   (Time)

Action Steps for Learning

Action 1: Set Goals

I'll bet you didn't see that coming! Don't worry if your goals are perfect, too wimpy, or too aggressive. Just write them down. One-month goals. One-year goals. Five-year goals. Ten- to fifteen-year goals. Goals in each of the eight domains (Family, Social, Religious/Spiritual, Health, Career, Financial, Intellectual/ Learning, Leisure). Write them down!

Action 2: Review Your Goals Regularly

After you had a chance to write down your goals, review them regularly. For goals that are for one year or less, I'd recommend reviewing them weekly. That way, you can see how to structure your upcoming week to pick off a few goals. For goals that are for greater than one year, I'd recommend reviewing them annually or a few times a year.

Action 3: Never Give Up on Your Dream

Sure, tangible goals are nice, but you also need a dream. If you don't have one, get one. If your dream is to have a have $10 million in the bank or a big house, that's not your dream. Those are desires. They can even be set as goals, but they're not your dream. Your dream involves you being involved in a community, doing something meaningful, and having a positive impact. Those are the elements for your dream. It is up to you to dream that dream.

Notes on Other Actions

What other actions could you take?

Word Problems: Vision = ?

A big audacious goal that I've been thinking about a lot is...

The fears which I must acknowledge around setting authentically daring goals are...

Vision:
How will I define success?

If I were to achieve my audacious goal, I would feel...

The three things which, if they happened, would make this year successful are...

DOMAIN: PURPOSE

Variable 9 =
PROCESS

- - - - - - - - - - - - - -

WHAT IS MY NEXT STEP?

You will never change your life until you change something you do daily. The secret of your success is found in your daily routine.

~Darren Hardy

What is my next step?

Enjoying the scents and sounds of my favorite coffee shop by the University of Michigan Medical School, I was looking forward to the good cup of joe and a conversation with the quiet and thoughtful young man sitting across from me.

"So, what interests you in medicine?" I asked, sipping my coffee.

"Many things actually. I'm not sure what to go after exactly…" His voice drifted with his thoughts as he searched, and I took another sip. "I think the interface of technology and medicine as a general direction. Yeah, I think that's the general direction."

"That's great. Tell me more…" I coaxed and then sat back to listen and ask questions over the next thirty minutes.

He shared that he had been involved in a few projects in medicine and technology and reflected on his interest relating to those projects. We talked about the future and what opportunities existed, including the possibilities of telemedicine—where instead of going to the clinic, you'd talk to a doctor on the phone. (This was in the days where telemedicine was still an emerging idea.)

"Yes, I'm really excited about this path, and I'm looking forward to becoming a leader in this new industry."

Wow, young people are so much more well-put-together these days. They're so intentional and accomplished. I was not like that when I was at that age, I thought to myself as I listened to him. *Of course, their icons in society are people like Mark Zuckerberg and other tech entrepreneurs who made their billions early in life, so there's much more pressure on them to become overnight successes. There are so many more resources, tips, and "tricks" about how to "optimize" the current stage of life. I'm sure it can be overwhelming.*

"Well, I can definitely see you becoming a leader in the industry. If you get up right now and march to the library and spend two hours learning as much as you can about telemedicine, you'd know more about telemedicine than 50% of the faculty here. In two hours a week for a month in the library learning about telemedicine, you'd probably know more about telemedicine than 90% of the faculty here. And if you spend two hours a week for four years while you are in medical school learning about telemedicine, you'd probably be one of the top ten people at this school in knowledge about telemedicine. You might even be able to start your own company about telehealth right out of med school."

I smiled as his eyes lit up with the possibility.

"Look, the truth is that most people see the overnight success of leaders in industries and want to know the "tips," "tricks," or "shortcuts." But the reality is that it takes preparation to become an overnight success. It takes a sustained effort towards something. You won't notice much in a week or in a month. However, over years (and not even that many years), you will notice a huge transformation. It begins by putting in a little effort. Over time, the little effort builds who you are and your vision for the future." I took another sip of coffee and waited for his response.

"Thanks, Mr. Tsai. I have felt a lot of pressure to do this all at once, but you're right. I know that it takes time and effort, and I'm willing to put them both into the process."

"I know you are, and I'm looking forward to seeing you enjoy the process a little more without all of the pressure. Now… let's talk about the game this Saturday against Michigan State…"

You are the sum of the little things.

Whatever you are, you're the sum of your experiences, days lived, genetics, and all of the potential things you may do, say, and feel. You are the effect you will have on other people.

You're also your habits, and your habits are all made of many micro-habits, even if you're not aware of them. We're always evolving, and we're always teaching ourselves how to evolve.

Another way to say this is that you improve at whatever you do. You're always getting better at something, even if it's getting better at getting worse. If you're like most of us, for instance, you probably sit in a chair for the majority of the day. Unless you spend a commensurate time standing, stretching, putting your shoulders back, and stretching your hip flexors to counteract the contractions of the sitting position, you'll wind up shaped like a chair. The guy in the gym who does nothing but bench press will eventually be shaped like the bench press. If you eat donuts regularly, you will soon resemble someone who eats donuts regularly. If you run every day, and you constantly challenge yourself, your lungs, body composition, and resting heart rate will all follow your lead.

If this sounds too obvious, consider that many of us already know things that would make us healthier or happier. And yet, we don't always prioritize them. Sometimes that's because we picture the end result that would make us happy, and it seems so far away that it barely seems worth pursuing.

Imagine that you've made a goal to run a 5K. But maybe you don't love the idea of running, you just love the idea of *having* run a 5K. You think that would make you happy. But at this moment, you aren't sure you could even run 500 meters without sending yourself to the morgue. You could, however, set yourself a small goal, every day for a week, of running for 400 meters. Then, add another 100 meters. Then another. Over a long enough time frame, you can scale up to a 5K length.

And yet, at the beginning of the process, your lungs may burn, your feet may hurt, and you may think: "Hey! Is anything even happening here?"

Yes, but the early differences may be invisible. Calluses begin to form on the soles of your feet. Your knees learn to absorb the impact of the road, and to adjust accordingly to lessen stress with each step. It may be a week, or a month later, but as with any practice that rewards stability and accumulation, you'll eventually hit a point where you say, "Hey! Something is happening!"

Depending on the path you choose, this can be a payoff for your effort, or a punishment that sets you back as habits all catch up with you at once.

Alas, very few worthwhile things happen all at once. You've probably heard the popular theory that it takes 10,000 hours to become a master at something. While you'll find those who swear by this, you'll find just as many who say it's bunk. But it's indisputable that mastery takes a long time. Big goals take big effort. If you want to spend ten years mastering running to the tune of 10,000 hours, it will require you to engage with it for approximately three hours per day. That's a substantial commitment, but mastery takes diligence, strength, patience, and a long-term perspective.

As a single footstep will not make a path on the earth, so a single thought will not make a pathway in the mind. To make a deep physical path, we walk again and again. To make a deep mental path, we must think over and over the kind of thoughts we wish to dominate our lives. ~ Henry David Thoreau

Think about something you want to master. Now consider how you would put 10,000 hours into it. There are lots of options.

You could read a book on your subject.

You could teach. There are few better ways to know whether you understand something than to challenge yourself to teach it to someone else. Mentoring and coaching are wonderful litmus tests for your own comprehension.

You could attend workshops and network with likeminded individuals who are striving for similar aims.

You could write out your ideas. Writing will often teach you what your opinions and beliefs are, or whether you even have them!

You could challenge your own reasoning and rhetoric and try to find the holes in your own arguments.

You could reach out to anyone who could serve as an ally, collaborator, or like-minded friend.

You could contemplate your goals, quietly observing your thoughts about them, trying to spot the patterns.

There are always options. There's always something that can be done to fill your 10,000 hours.

In these ways, the distance between dreams and reality diminishes via the process of discipline.

A formidable Navy SEAL named Jocko Willink recently published a book called *Extreme Ownership: How U.S. Navy SEALs Lead and Win.*[34] Jocko is in the habit of waking up every morning at 4:30 and sharing a picture of his digital watch on Twitter. It's not just to make everyone else feel lazy. It's so that he can demonstrate the power of his habits. Besides not getting enough sleep, his other pursuits include Jiu-Jitsu, surfing, strength training, and building his consulting company.

But the rallying cry behind them all is the same: "Discipline is freedom."

It might seem counterintuitive. Isn't the rigidity of a structure less-than-free by its nature? One common critique of systems is that they are systems, implying a built-in degree of ossification. Isn't part of blazing our own trail about making choices?

Yes. But making the right choices is even more important. Now, here's the truly counterintuitive point, at least at first.

If you develop habits, you don't have to make choices. That can be a real luxury. I know that sounds weird, but if you're serious about pursuing your goals with single-minded purpose, then having fewer choices will serve you well.

So, why is that?

Habit is greater than willpower.

Although she might appear to have little in common with Jocko Willink, in her book *Better Than Before: What I Learned About Making and Breaking Habits,* author Gretchen Rubin talks about the finite nature of willpower.[35]

When we try to make choices that will require effort—for instance, 99% of New Year's Resolutions—we make the assumption that it's a simple matter of willpower. We'll stick to it if we truly want it, and if we don't, then oh well, guess we'll try again next year.

But Rubin presents a great deal of persuasive data suggesting a more complicated reality. Willpower is a resource; and every time you make a choice, you deplete your reservoir. Imagine that today you wanted a donut 500 times, and all 500 times, you chose not to eat one. Well, by the time you get home tonight, all of the effort you put into resisting may make it easier for you to make a different poor choice. Maybe you skipped the donuts but you stayed up too late because that choice seemed too hard to resist. Or perhaps you had a glass of wine even though this was a day when you told yourself you wouldn't drink. But you do it because it feels like you can't resist. And, given the amount of choices you had to make with the donuts—choices that depended on willpower—maybe you can't resist! It's like trying to move a limb that has fallen asleep. You know it should work, but it just doesn't.

Once you ingrain a habit, you'll expend less energy trying to make the right choices. Anything that's truly a choice assumes the possibility of choosing wrong. Strong habits—as long as they're habits that serve our interests—are as close as we can get to working on our goals in a "set it and forget it" fashion.

If this sounds good, you might still be unsure how to get started. Your first impulse is probably to come up with a plan, step by step, of what will get you from here to there.

There's nothing wrong with a plan. However, as the scholar Alfred Korzybski famously said, "The map is not the territory." He was referring to the gap between belief and reality. Even the best plan is not enough. You have to have action as well. Some of our greatest writers work from outlines. But they'd be the first to admit that the plan isn't what makes it happen, and that their plans can go astray.

Those writers would also tell you that the best plan wouldn't do a thing for them if they never sat down to write. It's the literary equivalent of Newton's first law, which states that an object will remain at rest or continue to move at a constant velocity, unless acted on by an outside force. Nothing breaks itself out of inertia; it must be given a nudge.

When it comes to forming habits, the first nudge you should give yourself is to engage your emotions. Specifically, in order to bring about real, lasting change, it's critical to figure out exactly what you're dissatisfied with. Chasing a goal because you want it might not be as effective—in the beginning—as figuring out just what you're desperately unhappy with. Your emotions point the way to the habits that are most worth cultivating.

Consider the case of Maya Angelou, one of literature's great luminaries. There are passionate, aspiring authors who would give anything to be able to write like her, and to reach people with even an ounce of her influence. If any writer has ever been truly beloved, it's Maya Angelou. But even though she was gifted, perhaps unnaturally so, she wrote her books just like anyone else. Letters became words. Words became sentences. Sentences became paragraphs, paragraphs became pages, and, as days became years, pages become books.

She rarely deviated from her routine. After her morning coffee, Angelou would commute to the place where she would work (always in hotel or motel rooms). When she was finished writing, she would read the day's new text to herself. After showering, she would make dinner, and then read what she had written to her husband. That, combined with her life experience and her talent, was the secret to Maya Angelou's prolific career. It didn't require a minute-to-minute breakdown of her tasks.[36]

Call it a schedule, call it a ritual, call it whatever makes sense to you, but the best thing to call it consistency.

When he rose each morning, Benjamin Franklin would ask himself a simple question: "What good shall I do today?" After bathing, he would prepare his mind for the day's activities and ensure that he understood his schedule. After studying whatever occupied his interest at the moment, he went to work. After working for the first block of the day, he looked over his accounts or read, often while dining. Then he would work for another brief period. When the day's toil was officially over, he would put everything he had used back in its proper place. Evenings were spent with music, conversation, and reflections on the day.

Before sleeping, he would ask himself another simple question: "What good have I done today?" Then, to sleep. The next day, it was up and at 'em again. Day after day after day. [37]

My own daily routine—which I'm always willing to revise, based on the results I'm getting—is divided into morning and evenings blocks. (Please take this as one of many potential daily routines, not as a template or a suggestion that you mimic my schedule.)

When I wake up, I like to spend some time reflecting on purpose and gratitude. The morning is a time for me to ponder whether, and how, I am serving what I see as divine purpose. I eventually zero in on the power focus of the day. For example, on Monday, my power focus is career. On Tuesday, its's financial. On Wednesday, it's health. Then I attach a power focus activity for the day. For example, on Wednesdays, when I focus on health, I try to eat only healthy foods and I exercise more. Next, I identify, or reaffirm, three hours' worth of mission activities for the day. I think of an application of a core leadership idea. For example, on Thursday, the day which has the core leadership idea of "learning and mastery," I try to read books outside my traditional reading topics. Finally, to end the daily routine, I affirm that the divine is at work in my life.

In the evening, similarly to how Benjamin Franklin revisited his accounts, and how Maya Angelou reread her writing, I review my day and do my best to summarize it in one sentence. Whenever there is doubt or confusion, it's wise to look to the language being used. I find that reducing my day to a sentence distills the essence of my activities in a way that's impossible for me to misunderstand.

Next, I identify something about the day for which I am grateful.

I rate myself on my mission, my performance as a family member, my personal growth, and how much I am challenging myself.

I review what will happen tomorrow.

I request guidance on an issue. For me, this means prayer. For you, it could be talking with a mentor.

Finally, I read something inspirational. I define inspirational reading as anything that is most likely to galvanize me into action or new and challenging modes of thought.

I do these things every day. At this point, they do not happen because of my choices. They happen because I did them enough times to form them into habits.

Ralph Waldo Emerson said…

> *Sow a thought and you reap an action; sow an act and you reap a habit; sow a habit and you reap a character; sow a character and you reap a destiny.*

Are my habits going to lead me to my destiny? Well, what else would? (Please refer to the worksheet "Establishing Your Routines" at the end of this section.)

Emerson's quote is both an exquisitely sophisticated and incredibly simple crystallization of what the right habits can do. They can lead you towards your destiny.

So, how do we do it?

We start by getting rid of that pesky word, "How."

Don't worry about the *HOW.*

From now on you have one job: Focus on the *WHY*, not the *HOW.* As of this moment, the *HOW* is no longer any of your business.

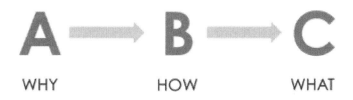

This might sound like a cop out. What do you mean that the *HOW* is none of my business?

So often, we are obsessed with formulas, the *HOW of things*. How do I start a company? How do I find a job? How do I get into a good grad school program? We neglect the *WHY* as well as the *WHAT*—the vision that we are trying to fulfill. We just want to follow a recipe for success, the way we did when we were children.

Why We Follow Recipes

While young, your ideas about what is good, right, and necessary are probably influenced by what your parents, teachers, and society has deemed good, right, and necessary. By definition, the inner voice of the young is less developed than in later years.

Young adulthood presents most people with the first experience of what Marcia Baxter Magolda calls the "crossroads." The crossroads is where the inner voice of the young adult is finally strong enough to question the voice of external authority. It's when the inner voice says "I hear you, but I have something to say as well, whether it's ultimately right or not."

Unfortunately, it's easiest to see the crossroads in hindsight. It's rarely a lightning bolt or a moment of insight that you can then weigh every subsequent decision and quandary against. Navigating the crossroads consists of the thousands of little and large decisions where you sit with confusion and ambivalence between two choices: what your inner voice is saying and the voice of external authority.

This is why it's so much easier to just focus on the *HOW* to get into med school than *WHY* to go to med school in the first place, or *WHAT* kind of doctor you intend to be.

The Only HOW You Need

The only way to real meaningful happiness based on *your* values and desires is to focus on clarifying your *WHY* and defining your *WHAT through action and intention.* This process is like an experiment.

Think about dating. To find a mate, you have to put yourself out there, with all the attendant highs and lows that entails. This is one of the arenas where you might learn that what you thought you wanted isn't what you actually want. That list of perfect attributes that your ideal mate was going to have might be swept away in some inexplicable chemistry with a person who takes your breath away, and barely resembles your initial vision.

Of course, if you don't get out there and experiment, experience won't shape you and help you clarify your true ideals. Experimenting, and all of its feedback, is how you become. This is how you close the gap between where you and where you want to be. With action and intention.

In taking the emphasis off of the *HOW*, this is not me encouraging you to shirk your responsibilities and roll the dice, leaving everything to fate and sending your plans into the paper shredder. I am simply saying that we have much less control over the future than we think. We plan and we plan, but events have a reasoning of their own that we often don't understand. (Please see the "Dog Analogy" later in this chapter) When this happens, understanding the *WHY* of the moment informs our current actions. So, this is me urging you to focus on what you can do right *now* to guarantee success.

> *Use human means as if there were no divine ones, and divine means as if there were no human ones.* ~ Baltasar Gracian

Every second is a choice. Every choice presents many opportunities and paths, but action in the moment is more likely to reward you than indecision because at least action provides feedback. Taking right actions now—or actions that are likely to contribute to your ultimate goal—is the crux of ensuring that the *HOW* takes care of itself.

Choices Lead to Results and Character

Humans are comprised of many selves. There are doubtful versions of us, and versions that are hard charging go-getters. There are versions who cling to guilt and others who treat ourselves with the compassion we want from others. However, the versions of us that get to spend the most time on stage, influencing our course, are the ones that we ultimately become in our lives.

There's a story I love that drives this point home:[38]

An old Cherokee is teaching his grandson about life. "A fight is going on inside me," he said to the boy.

"It is a terrible fight and it is between two wolves. One is evil—he is anger, envy, sorrow, regret, greed, arrogance, self-pity, guilt, resentment, inferiority, lies, false pride, superiority, and ego."

He continued.

"The other is good—he is joy, peace, love, hope, serenity, humility, kindness, benevolence, empathy, generosity, truth compassion, and faith. The same fight is going on inside you—and inside every other person, too."

The grandson thought about it for a moment and then asked his grandfather, "Which wolf will win?"

The old Cherokee simply replied, "The one you feed."

You can choose which wolf you feed. That choice is what gets you from A, your starting point, to C, your goal, without getting bogged down in between with details that you can't control. And once you do this a couple of times, really seeing it through, you'll learn to trust the process. You'll recognize your doubts about *HOW* for what they are: the wrong wolf to feed.

Success is not to be pursued; it is to be attracted by the person you become.

~ Jim Rohn

> **Key Lesson:** *Start taking action today.*
>
> **Key Points:**
> - *You are the sum of the little things.*
> - *Habit is greater than willpower.*
> - *Don't worry about the HOW.*

Action Steps for Learning

Action 1: Wake Up at a Regular Time

Set a time. 6:00 am? 7:00 am? 8:23 am? It doesn't matter. When you wake up at a regular time, it begins to put your whole body into a rhythm. If possible, routinize the first thirty minutes of your day. It also helps preserve your stamina for making decisions because you don't waste a lot of energy worrying about trivial things like when you should get up.

Action 2: Plan Your Week

Before your week starts (or at the beginning of the week), review your schedule. There are 168 hours in that week. Think about the most important things to get done in that time frame Three to five things. Block out the time in your 168 hours to do those. Then hold those times sacrosanct. In writing this book, I had to block out a number of hours every week for writing. In time, the book was completed.

Action 3: Inventory Your Activities

Every once in a while (e.g. monthly), take an inventory of how you spend your time. See if some bad habits have crept in. Monitor especially time on social media, video games, and TV. In the professional environment, monitor the projects and meetings you are involved with. Think to yourself: What are the three things I need to do less of in order to make time for the three things I need to do more of?

Notes on Other Actions

What other actions could you take?

"The Dog Analogy"
The Limits of Human Control

Think about a dog—we'll say it's your dog—and everything it knows. This is much easier than quantifying a human's internal inventory. Your dog's horizons, however wonderful the dog is, are not as expansive. What does a dog know? It knows the way its house smells. The sound of your voice. It knows the sight of its food dish and the feel of its bed. Perhaps it recognizes the sound of your footsteps coming up the walk when you get home from work, or the beeping of your car when you push the button of a key fob. The rattle of its leash. Combined with the sensations of hunger, thirst, fatigue, and all of the other things that all living beings experience, that might be it.

Here's what your dog doesn't know: Next Tuesday it's getting a shot at the vet. Today it's romping around, playing, eating, and just being a dog. It has no concept of tomorrow, let alone Tuesday. If it's been to the vet before, it has no concept of the veterinary office as a place where animals are healed. It's probably just a place that smells like a lot of animals.

So next Tuesday comes and you and your dog go to the vet. To your dog, this Tuesday trip has been the height of randomness and chaos. The dog just doesn't "get" what's happening, or how life has taken such a mad turn.

Your experience is different. When Tuesday arrives, for you, things could not be more predictable and routine. You made the appointment with a phone call or an email. You probably entered the appointment into a calendar. You put the leash on the dog, put the dog in the car, and made the infinite amount of micro-decisions required to navigate the roads and arrive.

Compared to you, your dog is operating on a lower level of order, or consciousness. You have the ability to reorganize your reality to make this trip to the vet possible. As humans, we seem to be at the top of the pile when it comes to controlling events. But there are things we can't, and will never be able to, control.

You can't even control who you may bump into on your way to work tomorrow. No matter how good of a driver you are, or how focused you're willing to be, you can't control whether anyone else on the road is practicing good habits and using their brains. In 2008, the financial crisis in America caused obscene amounts of damage, loss, hassle, and heartbreak. It happened because people lost control. It is these uncontrollable events that cause inordinate amounts of stress. They are unpredictable, random, and hard to understand. They're what that trip to the vet is for your dog.

Sometimes random things seem to occur in our lives, but are they really random? Could they just be events that we don't currently have enough information to understand?

Consider where man was 10,000 years ago. Something like a thunderclap would have seemed like random chaos to him. Today, thunder has a simple explanation. Yet there are many other things in our lives that seem random and chaotic, which may eventually have explanations as simple as the thunder.

We have two options for how we view humankind's place at the top of the pile: We can either say that we have achieved, in the present moment, the highest level of order and understanding there is or will ever be, or we can concede that there are still higher levels of understanding that we don't currently access, in the same way that a dog can't access the concept of Tuesday.

At some point, it's useful to concede that we are also the dog.

We are not fully in control, even though we'd like to think that we are. That's why we have this need to know. However, there is something going on that's larger than our ability to know. What's going on may seem random to us in this larger game/ order/God, force (whatever you choose to know it by), but isn't random when viewed through the lens of "full understanding." You ARE loved. You DO have a purpose. Trust in that as much as you can; have faith and act accordingly.

But you do not see, nor do you hear, and it is well.
The veil that clouds your eyes shall be lifted by the hands that wove it,
And the clay that fills your ears shall be pierced by those fingers that kneaded it.
And you shall see
And you shall hear.
Yet you shall not deplore having known blindness, nor regret having been deaf.
For in that day you shall know the hidden purposes in all things,
And you shall bless darkness as you would bless light.
~ Kahlil Gibran, *The Prophet*

Worksheet: Establishing Your Routines

A Daily Routine

In the space below, write down some habits or routines you can establish on a daily basis.

	Morning Routine What are some empowering things you can do to start your day?
	Midday Routine What are some empowering things you can do during the day?
	Evening Routine What are some empowering things you can do to end your day?

A Weekly Routine

In the space below, write down some habits or routines you can establish on a weekly basis.

Day of the Week	Habit / Routine
Monday	
Tuesday	
Wednesday	
Thursday	
Friday	
Saturday	
Sunday	

Word Problems: Process = ?

The three actions I could take this week to bring me closer to my goals are...

The three habits I need to develop in my life are...

Process:
What is my next step?

The three people I will tell about my goals, who can hold me accountable are...

The three things I need to do less of in order to make time for working on my goals are...

Developing Your Unique Formula: the PURPOSE Domain

MISSION

Question 9: ***What am I committed to that is greater than myself?***

> *The answer to this question is explored in the MISSION chapter.*

+

VISION

Question 10: ***How will I define success?***

> *The answer to this question is explored in the VISION chapter.*

+

PROCESS

Question 11: ***What is my next step?***

> *The answer to this question is explored in the PROCESS chapter.*

=

PURPOSE

Question 12: ***How will I contribute to the world around me?***

> *Recommendation: Answer this question after you have answered questions 9 to 11 as a synthesis of the answers from those supporting questions.*

THE OTHER HALF

--- --- --- --- --- --- --- --- ---

THE DEVELOPMENT OF MASTERY

The only person who is educated is the one who
has learned how to learn and change.

~ CARL ROGERS

All of this talk about meaning and purpose is not to minimize the importance of knowledge and skills. It's still important to know stuff. The world works because pilots know how to fly, surgeons can remove those tumors, experts keep the power grid working, teachers teach, chefs know how to cook, and so on. Expertise is not trivial.

The process of developing effective expertise is not *just* rote memorization of an endless list of information. How much do information do you retain after a test? It is not *just* doing problem sets over and over. How well can you apply problems in the problem sets to real-world situations?

Practice and repetition are indeed important, but must be balanced with a strategic perspective. This perspective is aligned with three domains: key knowledge, standards of behavior, and skills and techniques.

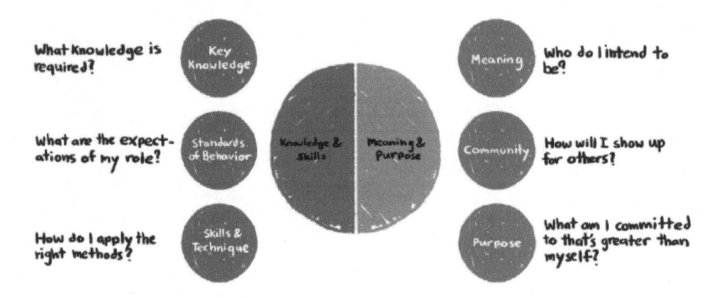

Each of these three domains has a strategic perspective to be understood and appreciated. Let's explore using a scenario that some of us (ahem…me) have considered at one time in our lives.

Let's say you had just finished watching a James Bond movie, and were wondering, "How could I be like that? What would it take for me to drive a car with as much confidence and skill as he does?"

Clearly, I am not talking about driving the old Honda Accord to the grocery store. I'm talking about passing cars with inches of clearance, making hairpin turns on cliff-faced roads, never needing a map or a GPS, and still not getting turned around.

To drive a car with that much skill will take effort. What does that effort look like in these three domains?

Key Knowledge (make "sense" of information)

Prior to working at Ford Motor Company, I knew very little about cars. If you'd asked me what kind of car I had, I would have said I had a Honda Accord. If you were to press me further, I would have said that I had a *green* Honda Accord.

If one really wanted to be a James Bond-level driver, one would need to know more about cars than that.

While working at Ford, I realized that there was a whole language around cars. There are various systems of the car such as: engine, fuel, exhaust, cooling, lubrication, electrical, transmission, and chassis. Each system has components, and each component has characteristics that affect the performance of the system. Without getting into a lot of nerdy car talk, I'll just say that different cars have different personalities in terms of their acceleration, handling, braking, etc. It is this type and depth of knowledge one needs to drive many different kinds of cars expertly.

In any area that you are looking to master, there is a set of knowledge to be acquired. This set of knowledge is the language which allows you access to that world.

In the beginning, it's hard to make sense of all the information in an area. You can Google it, but you don't yet have the context or experience to evaluate the validity of the information that you find. You might need to take a beginner's course. You might need to talk to an expert who can help you make sense of things. You might need to read some books which are seminal to the field you are investigating.

The process is like venturing into unexplored territory and trying to make *sense* of something new. It's more than memorizing facts. When you memorize, you're really just learning how things look and sound and it's hard to have the higher perspective where things connect and make sense. In fact, true learning begins when you begin to recognize patterns. When you can spot the patterns, you start to see how something *works,* even though it works according to the rules.

In grade school, people told you what you needed to learn, and learning things there probably looked like rote memorization. *What was going to be on the test?* You crammed and you crammed. Two weeks after the test, what do you remember? Is this learning?

Even though this book focuses on meaning and purpose (and community), education *does* involve the acquisition of knowledge. Instead of brute force memorizing and regurgitating for a test, think of learning as a process to make *sense* of a new territory. You will need to occasionally elevate yourself from the weeds to take a higher perspective to consolidate what you know, plan, and draw new connections.

Reflection on Key Knowledge:

What knowledge do I already know a lot about?

What knowledge am I *interested* in knowing more about? (considering your interests and your purpose)

What knowledge do I *need* to know more about? (considering your interests and your purpose)

Standards of Behavior (know the "rules of the game")

Let's say you became a knowledge expert on cars. You know how they accelerate and how they handle. Is that enough to be James Bond driver?

Some years ago, my wife and I vacationed in Southern France. Driving there in our car, everyone seemed to drive *so* slowly! It felt as if we were always tailgating the French locals. Of course, we were the misfits. Does it really matter that it took seven extra minutes to get to another village? After a few days, we were able to become more "French" and absorbed their pace and style. In fact, it made for a much more enjoyable experience.

On another vacation, I was driving my rental BMW on the Autobahn in Germany. There, it felt like I was the slowest person in Europe. Everyone was whizzing by me like I was standing still. The only time I was travelling the same speed as everyone else was during the traffic jams. Clearly, there was a different set of rules about driving there than in pastoral France.

I've never driven in Italy, but as a pedestrian, it seems that the sidewalks are just an extension of the road. If someone needs to drive on the sidewalk to get somewhere, they will do that. In travelling to different countries and seeing how different people drive, I've come to see how driving is an expression of culture.

If you want to be effective in driving, it matters where you are. Each place has different rules. If you are out of place with those rules, you're more likely to get into an accident. In order to learn the rules (a.k.a. the culture) of a place, you must be observant and figure out how to act in harmony with the locals.

Likewise, every profession has rules, many of which are unwritten ones. Organizations have cultures. Industries have their own idiosyncratic lingo. For instance, in the car industry, we don't sell cars. We "move metal." Learning is more than gleaning knowledge from books and lectures. Learning is also about understanding the "rules of the game."

This will often involve keen observation and interaction with others. When I was sitting in a lecture hall with 300 other students, there wasn't really much learning going on. I had to go talk to other students and TA's to understand the real rules of the game. In any learning situation, there are the outwards facts, and then there are the unspoken rules of the game. Pay attention to uncover those unspoken rules.

Reflection on Standards of Behavior:

What 'game' am I playing? (e.g. academics, social, professional, etc.)

What are the 'rules' of this game? What gets rewarded? What kind of people 'win'?

Who can I learn from to better understand the 'rules'?

Skills and Techniques (develop "mastery")

A few years ago, I was listening to the radio on my way to work. The announcer asked a question that made me laugh. But then, I realized was deceptively profound. "If we all drive to work every day," he asked, "shouldn't all this practice make us better drivers?"

Most of us drive. Few of us are expert drivers. What we see as driving "practice" actually makes us worse. Even though we go through the motions, we're still fiddling with the radio, eating, trying not to spill coffee, and God forbid, checking email. We're not mindful. We aren't invested in improving our driving. We're commuting from point A to point B. It's not a challenge, so we don't grow.

So, what could you do to become an "expert" driver? First, you'd have to make a decision. You would probably need to drive a lot of different vehicles, in many types of conditions. You would want to experiment with routes and different speed limits and learn the widths and textures of various roads. You could take a defensive driving class and learn the driving laws in different states or countries. Maybe you could even commit to watching all—I think there are eight now—of the Fast and the Furious movies and try to see if anything about what they do feels realistic or useful at all.

Too many of us are "commuting" in life. We think that just because we put in the time on something, we "deserve" to be promoted, or to grow, or to learn. No. That's not how it happens. What if you approached your education as the task of learning to improve? Developing your expertise is as much a function of choice as it is a function of time. What do you want to be a world-class expert in ten years from now?

Reflection on Skills and Techniques:

What skills am I *interested* in developing mastery in? (considering your interests and your purpose)

What skills do I *need* to develop more proficiency in? (considering your interests and your purpose)

What commitment will I have towards practice?

College gives you a chance to measure things, and evaluate yourself, in ways that you've never availed yourself. There might not be a greater gift you can give yourself than to improve the rate at which you can improve; and at its best, college is a continual challenge that forces you to stretch. And if nothing else, you can help yourself *see* it as a continual challenge that forces you to stretch if you care enough to commit to improvement.

Education is not preparation for life. Education is life itself. ~ John Dewey

RESTORATION

BALANCE IN EDUCATION

We shall not cease from exploration, and the end of all our exploring will be to arrive where we started and know the place for the first time.

~ T. S. ELIOT

Comets have often been associated with omens of disaster. Halley's comet, arguably the most famous, generated great consternation among observers. Even as far back as 66 AD, the comet was linked by Roman historians as a harbinger of the fall of Jerusalem. People were terrified of the "meaning" of the comet.

That interpretation seems silly to us now. We know "better" now. But how did we come to know?

At some point, human consciousness advanced to a point where we were able to critically and objectively examine our subjective beliefs against observable and measurable phenomenon. We realized that Halley's comet was just a giant snowball that orbited the sun that came around every seventy-five years. It didn't *cause* anything. The *meaning* that we had formerly attributed to it was false.

It was like when we were kids and thought that there was a monster under the bed, but upon closer examination, it was just a giant dust bunny. The giant dust bunny didn't *mean* anything. We had to grow up and objectively examine our beliefs and shed the former structures of meaning that no longer serve us.

Human beings are still in this phase, albeit at the tail end. We have built tremendous structures of objective observation. These structures have given us great insight and power over the physical world. We have had to 'outgrow' our former internal structures of meaning in order to see things "objectively." This was necessary.

However, we're realizing that objectivity is empty without meaning. In the academic medical field, there are billions of dollars going towards scientific research. Perhaps we'll find a cure for all these ailments troubling people these days. Perhaps people will live another fifteen years longer. Well…so what? If one's life wasn't that meaningful to begin with, why live another fifteen years of it?

Yet, because of our inertia, we are still focused on acquiring more knowledge. This is perpetuated in the education system.

I live in the world of MDs and PhDs. They are some of the most educated people on earth. Yet, they experience tremendous amount of suffering and burnout. They know a lot. Yes. They know how to interpret a patient's test results. They know how to generate a differential diagnosis. They know whether a patient requires surgery. They know how to conduct groundbreaking research.

They are also quite ignorant of other things. They often struggle to articulate: why practicing medicine is meaningful, what their professional ethics and values are as a physician, what is their professional mission and how they will impact their profession.

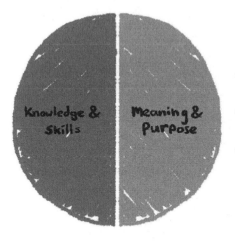

Example Questions

- How do I interpret a patient's blood test results?
- How do I generate a differential diagnosis?
- How do I determine whether a patient requires surgery?

Strategy: Acquire and Practice.

Knowledge & Skills

Meaning & Purpose

Example Questions

- Why is practicing medicine meaningful for me?
- What are my professional ethics and values as a physician?
- What is my professional mission and how will I impact the field of medicine?

Strategy: Experience and Reflect.

He who has a why to live can bear almost any how. ~ Friedrich Nietzsche

I think back to the time I spent in school. How many hours did I spent solving for the proverbial "X"? This "X" is not just the one in the algebra equations. It is anything that I needed to find the answer for outside of myself.

What is the capital of Pennsylvania? ... X

What years did the Civil War take place? ... X

What is the U.S. corporate tax rate? ... X

Why are manhole covers round? ... X

I had to search for answers outside of myself so often that I barely knew who I was. Sure, I had all these degrees to certify that I knew some things, but so what? Without a sense of meaning, purpose, and community, I couldn't live a life that was authentic to me.

That's when I realized that instead of solving for "X," I needed to solve for "WHY." I had to ask myself questions and look *inside* to find answers.

I had to ask myself:

Who do I intend to be?

I had to ask myself:

How will I show up for others?

I had to ask myself:

How will I contribute to the world around me?

Through persistent reflection, I was able to develop answers for myself which gives meaning, community, and purpose to my life. I realized that what I really wanted, and what we all want is *to contribute our unique gift, while finding belonging in a caring community, to something meaningful that is greater than ourselves.*

Meaning ↓
Community ↙
To contribute your unique gift, while finding belonging in a caring community, to something meaningful that is greater than yourself.
↖ Purpose

I believe it is the goal of education to help people actualize this statement. This requires both "halves" of education to be present. You DO need knowledge, and you DO need meaning. The current systems in higher education do a good job with one, but the other is up to you for now.

I hope the concepts and exercises in this book have helped you on your journey to create meaning, community, and purpose in your life.

The point is to become yourself, to use yourself completely – all your skills, gifts and energies – in order to make your vision manifest. You must withhold nothing. You, must, in sum, become the person you started out to be, and to enjoy the process of becoming. ~ Warren Bennis

Appendix - Summary of the MEANING Domain

To contribute your unique gift...

MEANING

- Question: *Who do I intend to be?*
- Lesson: *Stand for something*
- Key distinction: *Authenticity instead of imitation*

Topics in the MEANING domain

VALUES

- Question: *What matters most to me?*
- Lesson: *Know what is important*
- Key points:
  - ▶ *Your values are you, and you are your values*
  - ▶ *The most important choices are internal*
  - ▶ *Fulfillment comes from making choices consistent with your values*

STRENGTHS

- Question: *What could I do better than most others?*
- Lesson: Develop and *apply your talents*
- Key points:
  - ▶ *We're not wired to see "strengths"*
  - ▶ *Your strengths are the "real" you*
  - ▶ *Maximize the contribution of your unique gifts*

SELF-AWARENESS

- Question: *How do others see me, and how do I see myself?*
- Lesson: *Take a step back to reflect*
- Key points:
  - ▶ *Our lives are driven by our narratives*
  - ▶ *We can make our own meaning*
  - ▶ *Find time to reflect and learn from others' feedback*

Appendix - Summary of the COMMUNITY Domain

…while finding belonging within a caring community…

COMMUNITY

- Question: *How will I show up for others?*
- Lesson: *See the humanity in others*
- Key distinction: *Empathy instead of transaction*

Topics in the COMMUNITY domain

NETWORK

- Question: *What kind of people do I need to know?*
- Lesson: *Define and expand your social circle*
- Key points:
  - ▶ *You become more like the people you associate with*
  - ▶ *Different people contribute in different ways*
  - ▶ *"Invest" in your network*

RELATIONSHIPS

- Question: *What's my way to build connection with others?*
- Lesson: *Build trusting relationships*
- Key point:
  - ▶ *It's all about trust*
  - ▶ *Focus more on giving than getting*
  - ▶ *Love everyone (You can only work on yourself)*

COMMUNICATION

- Question: *How do I communicate with influence?*
- Lesson: *Speak the truth with compassion*
- Key point:
  - ▶ *Communication starts with your state*
  - ▶ *Know who you're communicating with, and empathize with them*
  - ▶ *Speak the truth with compassion*

Appendix - Summary of the PURPOSE Domain

…to something meaningful that is greater than yourself.

PURPOSE

- Question: *How will I contribute to the world around me?*
- Lesson: *Be a 'giver' and not a 'taker'*
- Key disctinction: *Contributing instead of consuming*

Topics in the PURPOSE domain

MISSION

- Question: *What am I committed to that is greater than myself?*
- Lesson: *Define your purpose*
- Key points:
  - ▶ *We exist to serve others*
  - ▶ *All problems are not the same*
  - ▶ *We each have something unique to contribute*

VISION

- Question: *How will I define success?*
- Lesson: *Set an intention and work towards it*
- Key point:
  - ▶ *Work expands so as to fill the time available for its completion (Parkinson's Law)*
  - ▶ *Begin with the end in mind*
  - ▶ *Push beyond your comfort zone*

PROCESS

- Question: *What is my next step?*
- Lesson: *Start taking action today*
- Key point:
  - ▶ *You are the sum of the little things*
  - ▶ *Habit is greater than willpower*
  - ▶ *Don't worry about the HOW*

NOTES

THE TWO HALVES OF THE EDUCATION EQUATION

1   Drucker, Peter F. *The essential Drucker : selections from the management works of Peter F. Drucker*. New York: HarperBusiness, 2001.

2   Northouse, Peter G. *Leadership : theory and practice*. Thousand Oaks: Sage Publications, 2010.

Domain: MEANING

(no notes)

Variable 1 = VALUES

(no notes)

Variable 2 = STRENGTHS

3   Drucker, Peter F. *The effective executive*. New York: Collins, 2006.

4   Rozin, Paul, and Edward B. Royzman. "Negativity Bias, Negativity Dominance, and Contagion." *Personality and Social Psychology Review*, vol. 5, no. 4, 2001, pp. 296–320.

5   Peterson, Jordan. "Past Authoring, Present Authoring, Future Authoring The Self Authoring Suite." *Selfauthoring.com*, selfauthoring.com/.

6   Rath, Tom. *Strengths finder 2.0*. New York: Gallup Press, 2007.

7   The four quadrants is based on the Comepting Values Framework: Cameron, Kim S. *Competing values leadership : creating value in organizations*. Cheltenham, UK Northampton, MA: E. Elgar Pub, 2006.

8   Hamblin, James. "The Physiological Power of Altruism." *The Atlantic*, Atlantic Media Company, 4 Jan. 2016, www.theatlantic.com/health/archive/2015/12/altruism-for-a-better-body/422280/.

Variable 3 = SELF-AWARNESS

9   Crum, Alia J., and Ellen J. Langer. "Mind-Set Matters." *Psychological Science*, vol. 18, no. 2, 2007, pp. 165–171.

10   Beck, Martha. "Victory by Surrender." *Marthabeck.com*, marthabeck.com/2011/09/victory-by-surrender/.

11   Ignatius, and George E. Ganss. *The spiritual exercises of Saint Ignatius : a translation and commentary*. St. Louis: Institute of Jesuit Sources, 1992.

12   Adler, Nancy J. "Want to Be an Outstanding Leader? Keep a Journal." *Harvard Business Review*, 13 Jan. 2016.

Domain: COMMUNITY

13   This concept of transaction versus relationship can be found from a number of sources. For me, the concept became clearer to me in discussions with a mentor of mine from the Ross School of Business at the University of Michigan, Bob Quinn. He's a well-respected scholar on the topic of leadership, and someone I personally admire. He taught a course on transformational leadership which I had the honor to participate in.

14   Murthy, Vivek. "Work and the Loneliness Epidemic." *Harvard Business Review*, Sept. 2017.

15   Baumeister, Roy F., and Mark R. Leary. "The Need to Belong: Desire for Interpersonal Attachments as a Fundamental Human Motivation." *Psychological Bulletin*, vol. 117, no. 3, 1995, pp. 497–529.

Variable 4 = NETWORK

16   Morin, Rich. "Is Divorce Contagious?" *Pew Research Center*, Pew Research Center, 21 Oct. 2013, www.pewresearch. org/fact-tank/2013/10/21/is-divorce-contagious/.

17   Christakis, Nicholas A., and James H. Fowler. "Social Contagion Theory: Examining Dynamic Social Networks and Humanâ‰Behavior." Statistics in Medicine, vol. 32, no. 4, 2012, pp. 556–577.

18   Grant, Adam M. *Give and take : why helping others drives our success*. New York: Penguin Books, 2014.

19   Rockquemore, Kerry Ann. "There Is No Guru | Inside Higher Ed." *Insidehighered.com*, Inside Higher Ed, 19 Apr. 2010, www.insidehighered.com/advice/2010/04/19/there-no-guru.

Variable 5 = RELATIONSHIPS

20   Grant, Adam M. *Give and take : why helping others drives our success*. New York: Penguin Books, 2014.

21   This concept was inspired after attending a weekend seminar called *The Breakthrough Experience* which was given by John Demartini. The concept of perfection and balance was something that he emphasized throughout the seminar. It is for us to pereceive this balance, which already exists.

Variable 6 = COMMUNICATION

(no notes)

Domain: PURPOSE

22   United States, Congress, Office of Land and Emergency Management. "Advancing Sustainable Materials Management: 2014 Fact Sheet." *Advancing Sustainable Materials Management. 2014 Fact Sheet*, 2016.

23   DiLallo, Matthew. "Here's How Much Gasoline the Average American Consumes Annually." The Motley Fool, The Motley Fool, 14 Jan. 2017, www.fool.com/investing/2017/01/14/heres-how-much-gasoline-the-average-american-consu.aspx.

24   Baldé, C.P., Wang, F., Kuehr, R., Huisman, J. (2015), *The global e-waste monitor – 2014*, United Nations University, IAS – SCYCLE, Bonn, Germany. ·

25   This concept was inspired through conversations with a colleague, Wiley ("Chip") Souba. We had discussed the fundamental importance of being committed to something greater than ourselves.

Variable 7 = MISSION

26   Omidyar, Pierre. "How Pierre Omidyar Turned of EBay An Idealistic Notion Into Billions Of Dollars." *Inc.com*, Inc., 9 Dec. 2013, www.inc.com/magazine/201312/pierre-omidyar/ebay-inspiration-more-effective-than-delegation.html.

27   "Our History." *EBay Inc.*, www.ebayinc.com/our-company/our-history/.

28   Ibid.

29   "Purpose, Vision, Values, and Mission." *Southwest Airlines*, investors.southwest.com/our-company/purpose-vision-values-and-mission.

30   "About - Microsoft." *Microsoft.com*, www.microsoft.com/en-us/about/default.aspx.

31   "About Us." *Teach For America*, 10 Apr. 2018, www.teachforamerica.org/about-us.

32   Cameron, Kim S. *Competing values leadership : creating value in organizations*. Cheltenham, UK Northampton, MA: E. Elgar Pub, 2006.

Variable 8 = VISION

33   Parkinson, Cyril Northcote. "Parkinson's Law". The Economist. London. 19 November 1955.

Variable 9 = PROCESS

34   Willink, Jocko, and Leif Babin. *Extreme ownership : how U.S. Navy SEALs lead and win*. New York: St. Martin's Press, 2017.

35   Rubin, Gretchen. *Better than before : mastering the habits of our everyday lives*. New York: Crown Publishers, 2015.

36   Currey, Mason, and Mason Currey. *Daily rituals : how artists work*. New York: Alfred A. Knopf, 2013.

37   Ibid.

38   "Two Wolves, A Cherokee Legend." *Native American Legends*, www.firstpeople.us/FP-Html-Legends/TwoWolves-Cherokee.html.

THE OTHER HALF

(no notes)

RESTORATION

(no notes)